IBC対訳ライブラリー

英語で読む 錦織圭
The Kei Nishikori Story

松丸さとみ 著
バーナード・セリオ 英訳
山本 裕也 英語解説

JN162962

まえがき

　本書は、現役のプロテニス・プレーヤー、錦織圭選手の半生の物語を通じて英語に触れ、英語力の向上を目指すものです。

　「好きこそものの上手なれ」と言いますが、自分の好きなものに取り組むときは、その努力自体が楽しく、苦にならずに続けられるものではないでしょうか。本書を手に取った皆さんはテニスが好きなのだと思いますが、テニスをプレイまたは観戦していると、きっとあっという間に時間が経ってしまうと感じることでしょう。同様に、好きなものを通じて英語に触れると、自然と楽しい時間が過ごせることと思います。英語自体が好き、という人も多いかもしれませんが、自分の好きな話題を英語で読めば、より楽しみながら英語に触れられ、単語や表現も覚えやすくなるのは間違いありません。

　ですので、ぜひ本書を通じて、テニスや錦織選手について、英語で熱く語れるようになっていただければと思います。そのためのボキャブラリーや表現は、本書の至るところで見つかるはずです。また、あなたが英語好きなら、英語でテニスや錦織選手について話すとき、ワクワクした感情が自分の中から湧き上がってくるのを感じるでしょう。そのワクワクを心から楽しんでください。

　私の場合、英語を「学業」と捉えていた学生時代は、英語の成績は良いとはお世辞にも言えませんでした。でも、英国で暮らしたと

きに、英語が学業ではなく「コミュニケーション・ツールの１つ」と気付いてから、英語が楽しくなりました。相手の言っていることを理解したい。相手に自分の考えや気持ちを伝えたい。そういう思いが英語力を向上させるエネルギーになりました。英語がゴールなのではなく、英語を使って何をしたいのか、明確にすることが、英語上達のカギだと思います。

　また、英語はリズムがあってとても楽しい言語です。本書を朗読しているCDは、聞くだけでなく、ナレーターの発音や抑揚を真似ながら実際に声に出して一緒に読んでみることをお勧めします。

　なお文末となりますが、本書の執筆にあたり巻末に掲載のメディア記事等を参考にいたしました。各メディアにお礼申し上げます。

松丸さとみ

スピーキングとライティングに役立つ
本書の活用術!!

1 まずは読んでみて、このセンテンスが好きとか、かっこいい、自分の口から言ってみたい、うまく言えそうにないなどといった部分にマーカーやチェックをしていきましょう。このときどのセンテンスや段落を選ぶかは自分の好みです。自分の感性に従いましょう。

2 次にその文章の単語の意味や文法を確認したあと、暗唱できるまで音読し、繰り返し発声しましょう。その際、本書付属のMP3を使って音声のまねをして読む（リピーティング）をしたり、シャドーイングをするとリスニングの力も上がります。ノートにまとめてもオッケーです。

3 最後に自分が実際にそのチェックした表現を使うときはどんな場面だろうということを考えましょう。ここをしっかり考えないと、せっかく覚えたのにも関わらず瞬時にアウトプットができないということが起こってしまいます。どうしても思い浮かばないときは、その表現をインターネットで調べて例文をストックするようにしましょう。

　このように私は英語学習の日課として純粋に読んで内容を楽しんだあと、自分の好きなワードや、フレーズ、感動したセンテンスなどをストックしています。この作業をしていると、まるで宝石探しの旅に行っているような気になります。
　ウォルト・ディズニーも以下の名言を残しています。

There is more treasure in books than in all the pirates' loot on Treasure Island.（宝島の海賊たちが盗んだものより、本の中には多くの財宝がある。）

　この名言は英語学習にも通じるものがあると思います。ぜひ読者の皆さまも自分だけの財宝を見つけていってください。I keep my fingers crossed for you!!!

山本 裕也

Yuya Yamamoto　福島県生まれ。青山学院大学教育人間科学部を卒業。その後、英国公的機関のBritish Councilが提供するIELTS奨学金 Study UK 2015を授賞し、英国バーミンガム大学大学院で「外国語としての英語教授法」(TEFL) 修士号を取得。専門は教師教育、モチベーション。実用英語検定1級。日本人の英語4技能（特にスピーキングとライティング）を伸ばすために、日々教授法を研究中。

本書の構成

本書は、

- ☐ 英日対訳による本文
- ☐ 覚えておきたい英語表現
- ☐ 欄外の語注
- ☐ MP3形式の英文音声

で構成されています。

本書は、テニスプレーヤー錦織圭の物語を英語／日本語で読み進めながら、同時に役立つ英語表現も学んでいけるように構成されています。

各ページの下部には、英語を読み進める上で助けとなるよう単語・熟語の意味が掲載されています。また英日の段落のはじまりが対応していますので、日本語を読んで英語を確認するという読み方もスムーズにできるようになっています。またストーリーの途中に英語解説がありますので、本文を楽しみながら、英語の使い方などをチェックしていただくのに最適です。

付属のCD-ROMについて

本書に付属のCD-ROMに収録されている音声は、パソコンや携帯音楽プレーヤーなどで再生することができるMP3ファイル形式です。一般的な音楽CDプレーヤーでは再生できませんので、ご注意ください。

■音声ファイルについて

付属のCD-ROMには、本書の英語パートの朗読音声が収録されています。本文左ページに出てくるヘッドホンマーク内の数字とファイル名の数字がそれぞれ対応しています。

パソコンや携帯プレーヤーで、お好きな箇所を繰り返し聴いていただくことで、発音のチェックだけでなく、英語で物語を理解する力が自然に身に付きます。

■音声ファイルの利用方法について

CD-ROMをパソコンのCD/DVDドライブに入れて、iTunesなどの音楽再生(管理)ソフトにCD-ROM上の音声ファイルを取り込んでご利用ください。

■パソコンの音楽再生ソフトへの取り込みについて

パソコンにMP3形式の音声ファイルを再生できるアプリケーションがインストールされていることをご確認ください。

CD-ROMをパソコンのCD/DVDドライブに入れても、多くの場合音楽再生ソフトは自動的に起動しません。ご自分でアプリケーションを直接起動して、「ファイル」メニューから「ライブラリに追加」したり、再生ソフトのウインドウ上にファイルをマウスでドラッグ＆ドロップするなどして取り込んでください。

音楽再生ソフトの詳しい操作方法や、携帯音楽プレーヤーへのファイルの転送方法については、ソフトやプレーヤーに付属のマニュアルで確認するか、アプリケーションの開発元にお問い合わせください。

Table of Contents

Chapter 1 : Laying the Foundations.................... *11*
From Birth to Going to the U.S.A. (1989–2003)

Chapter 2 : Anguish.................... *43*
Plagued by Injuries (2003–2010)

Chapter 3 : Restart.................... *89*
Meeting with Chang and Subsequent Advancement (2011–2014)

Chapter 4 : A Feat.................... *115*
Setting the Record as an Asian Male Player (2014)

Chapter 5 : The Future.................... *143*
Kei's Goals (2015–)

カバー写真 ＝ 長田洋平/アフロスポーツ
ナレーション ＝ Howard Colefield
録音スタジオ ＝ 株式会社巧芸創作

本書の英語テキストは、弊社から刊行されたラダーシリーズ
『The Kei Nishikori Story 錦織圭物語』と共通です。

目次

第1章:「基盤」..................................*11*
　生い立ち〜渡米まで (1989〜2003)

第2章:「苦悩」..................................*43*
　米国留学〜ケガで苦しんだ時期 (2003〜2010)

第3章:「再出発」................................*89*
　チャンとの出会いとその後の快進撃 (2011〜2014)

第4章:「快挙」..................................*115*
　アジア人男子初の記録 (2014)

第5章:「未来」..................................*143*
　錦織の目指すところ (2015〜)

覚えておきたい英語表現..................*40, 86, 112, 140, 172*

【錦織圭を囲む人々】

Nick Bollettieri（ニック・ボロテリー）
　IMGアカデミーの前身、ニック・ボロテリー・テニスアカデミー創立者。テニスコーチ。アガシやベッカー、シャラポワなど世界トップレベルの選手を育ててきた。

Olivier van Lindonk（オリビエ・ヴァン・リンドンク）
　圭のマネージャー。IMGアカデミーのテニス部門ヴァイス・プレジデント。

Michael Chang（マイケル・チャン）
　2013年末から圭のコーチ。元テニス選手。1989年の全仏オープンを17歳3ヵ月で優勝し、この最年少記録は2015年現在も破られていない。アメリカ、ニュージャージー州出身。

Dante Bottini（ダンテ・ボッティーニ）
　2010年から圭のコーチ。アルゼンチン出身の元選手。

【用語解説】

ATP: Association of Tennis Professionals（男子プロテニス協会）
　男子プロテニス・ツアーを統括、運営する団体。

ATP World Ranking（ATP世界ランキング）
　男子シングルスおよびダブルスのエントリー資格やシードを決定する際に使用される、直近の52週（1年間）18試合での戦績に基づき算出するランキング。ただし、ATPワールドツアー・ファイナルは別枠で加算される。
- グランドスラム4大会
- ATPワールドツアー1000トーナメント8大会
- ワールドツアー500
- ワールドツアー250、ATPチャレンジャー・ツアー、フューチャーズ・トーナメント

Grand Slam（グランドスラム）
　以下の4大大会の総称。またはこの4大大会すべてを制すること。
- 全豪オープン（1月）（ハードコート）
- 全仏オープン（5月／6月）（クレーコート）
- 全英オープン（6月／7月）（グラスコート）
- 全米オープン（8月／9月）（ハードコート）

　優勝者には2000ポイントが付与される。

The Kei Nishikori Story

Chapter 1
Laying the Foundations
From Birth to Going to the U.S.A. (1989–2003)

第1章
「基盤」
生い立ち〜渡米まで（1989〜2003）

Kei was born in Matsue, Shimane prefecture on December 29, 1989. Facing the Japan Sea, the slow-paced city of Matsue is an old castle town which also features in Japanese mythology. At present, its population is slightly more than 200,000.

When Kei was five, his father Kiyoshi, who was an engineer, bought a children's tennis racket as a present for him when he went to America on a business trip. This was when Kei first encountered tennis. Then Kei became familiar with tennis and really got into it—he played with his father or sister, and sometimes he hit the ball against a wall.

Other children who had just started playing tennis could not even hit a ball with the racket. But Kiyoshi says Kei was able to hit it back at the age of five. Both Kiyoshi and his wife Eri had belonged to a tennis circle at college but they had never played tennis seriously. But the couple recognized their son's talent and sent him to a local tennis school, the Green

■prefecture 名県 ■face 動面する ■feature in 〜に登場する ■mythology 名神話 ■encounter 動出会う ■become familiar with 〜に慣れ親しむ ■get into 〜にのめり込む ■talent 名才能

錦織は1989年12月29日、島根県松江市で生まれた。松江市は日本海に面し、城下町や神話の町としても知られる、人口わずか20万人強ののんびりとした地域だ。

　錦織が5歳のとき、父親でエンジニアの清志が出張でアメリカに行った際に、お土産に子供用のテニス・ラケットを買ってきた。錦織がテニスと出会った瞬間だった。それ以来、錦織は父や姉と打ち合ったり、壁打ちをしたりしてテニスに親しみ、次第にテニスにのめり込んでいった。

　テニスを始めたばかりの子供なら普通、ボールをラケットに当てることすらままならないだろう。しかし清志によると、錦織は5歳の時点ですでにボールを打ち返すことができていたという。清志も母の恵理もテニスは大学時代にサークルでやっていた程度で本格的にプレーしたことはなかった。しかし息子にテニスの才能を感じた2人は、錦織が6歳のときに地元の「グリーンテニススクール」に通わせるようになった。清志は仕事

Tennis School, when he became six. On weekends, Kiyoshi took Kei to and from the school by car; he extended full support to his tennis.

Masaki Kashiwai, the head coach of the Green Tennis School who instructed Kei, recalls that Kei often challenged and defeated older boys when he was an elementary school kid. Kashiwai says, "He had ball control that only one player in 100 has and a knack for the game that only one in 100 has. So all in all, he was one in 10,000 players."

Also, the school's coach Kiyomi Kashiwai recalls Kei's fascination with tennis. When he was an elementary school kid, he had a finger injury. When Kiyomi advised him to stop training, he replied, "If I am deprived of tennis, soccer and video games, it's like I'm being told to die." She remembers she had a feeling that Kei was indeed aiming to be number one in the world.

■take someone to and from（人を）〜まで送り迎えする　■extend 動（援助などを）与える　■recall 動思い起こす　■knack for 〜の才覚　■all in all 全体として　■deprive 動奪う

が休みの週末は車でテニススクールに送り迎えするなどして、錦織のテニスを全面的にサポートした。

　グリーンテニススクールで錦織を指導した柏井正樹ヘッドコーチによると、小学生のとき錦織はすでに、自分より年上の選手を相手にし、よく負かしていたという。柏井は錦織について、「ボールコントロールのよさは100人に1人。試合運びの才覚は100人に1人。つまり1万人に1人の逸材」と評価している。

　また、柏井貴代美コーチは錦織について、とにかくテニスが大好きだった姿を記憶している。錦織が小学生のときに、指にケガをしたことがあった。貴代美コーチが錦織に練習を休むよう諭すと、「ボクからテニスとサッカーとゲームを取ったら、死ねということだ」と言ったそうだ。同コーチは、このころからすでに世界一を本気で考えていたようだった錦織の姿を記憶しているという。

Kei was also a leading player at the soccer club of the elementary school. But it seems that he was determined to be a professional tennis player. He preferred individual sports rather than team sports because the result of the game was entirely up to him.

At the age of seven, Kei, accompanied by his mother Eri, visited a local cram school. He wanted to study English so that he could play tennis abroad in the future. The owner of the cram school was impressed with his zest. Most children who wanted to be tennis players would just play tennis. But Kei was different. As an elementary school kid, he already understood that he needed to study English to be a world-class tennis player. This led the owner to offer a course for young children at his school, which had had only high-school-level classes until then.

■leading 形 主要な　■individual 形 個人の　■up to ～次第で　■be accompanied by ～が同伴する　■cram school 塾　■so that ～できるように　■zest 名 熱意
■offer 動 (～のために) 用意する

錦織は、小学校のサッカーチームでも中心選手になっていた。しかしこのころはすでに、錦織はプロのテニス選手になる決意をしていたらしい。チームスポーツのサッカーではなく個人競技のテニスを選んだのは、勝つも負けるも自分次第だから、という理由だった。

　7歳のとき、錦織は母親の恵理に手を引かれて地元の塾を訪ねた。将来的に海外でテニスがプレーできるよう英語を習いたい、ということだった。塾の経営者は、その熱意に打たれた。普通の子供なら、テニスがしたいのならテニスだけに打ち込むところだが、錦織は、世界で活躍するなら英語を学ばなければいけないということを、小学生ながらすでに理解していたのだ。そのためこの経営者は、当時は高校生向けのクラスしかなかった塾で、子供向けのクラスを作るに至ったという。

Toward Being a Top Junior Tennis Player in Japan

Kei's enthusiasm for tennis bore its first fruit in 2001, when he won three major tournaments: the All-Japan Selected Junior Tennis Championship (U-12), All-Japan Elementary School Tennis Championship and All Japan Junior Tennis Championship (U-12). He became the fifth grand-slammer in history. In the same year, he was invited to the "Shuzo Challenge" offered by a former professional tennis player Shuzo Matsuoka.

The Shuzo Challenge is a tennis camp hosted by Shuzo Matsuoka, who achieved a career-high no. 46 in the ATP rankings. He started this initiative soon after he finished his tennis circuit in 1998. It involves a camp training program for developing junior tennis players aged from 10 to 18 years with the aim of helping young Asian players to achieve good results in Grand Slams or attain a Top 100 ranking.

■enthusiasm 名情熱 ■bear a fruit 実を結ぶ ■championship 名選手権 ■grand-slammer 名主要な大会すべてで優勝した人 ■former 形かつての ■ATP 略プロテニス選手協会《Association of Tennis Professionals》 ■initiative 名新たな取り組み ■circuit 名巡業試合

日本を代表するジュニア選手へ

　錦織のテニスへの情熱はまず2001年、小学校6年生のときに、全国選抜ジュニアテニス選手権（U12）、全国小学生テニス選手権、全日本ジュニアテニス選手権12歳以下の3大大会での優勝という形で実を結んだ。これら大会の三連覇は、史上5人目の快挙だった。さらにその年、プロテニス選手である松岡修造が主催する「修造チャレンジ」に招待された。

　「修造チャレンジ」とは、錦織がその記録を塗り替えるまで日本人男子として世界ランキング最高位の記録を保持していた松岡が、1998年にプロツアー選手を退いた直後に立ち上げた活動だ。10〜18歳のジュニア選手育成を目標とした強化キャンプで、グランドスラム大会で活躍したり、世界ランキング100位に入ったりできるような若きアジア人選手の輩出を目指している。

In the Shuzo Challenge, the 11-year-old, sixth-grader Kei beat a high-school student who was much older and better built than Kei. This match put him in the spotlight. Matsuoka is said to have recognized his potential at this point. (The high-school student defeated in that match was Tomohiro Ishii, who would become an announcer on TBS.)

The first impression Matsuoka had when he first met Kei was that he was not physically conspicuous, but seemed prodigious on the tennis court.

Matsuoka recalls that he was quite strict with Kei at that time. But Matsuoka never criticized his technique. Kei already had something special, so Matsuoka did not want him to lose it by changing his style. Matsuoka was very strict with Kei because he knew this boy would succeed.

To be a top player, one needs to be familiar with English and other cultures as well as good at tennis, Matsuoka adds. So the Shuzo Challenge offers training in self-expression in English as well as intensive practice in tennis.

■beat 動打ち負かす　■built 形体格のよい　■put ~ in the spotlight　~に脚光を浴びせる　■conspicuous 形目立つ　■prodigious 形並外れた　■as well as ~と同様にうまく　■intensive 形集中的な

この「修造チャレンジ」では、わずか11歳、小学校6年生だった錦織が、歳も体格も格段に違う高校生を相手に試合で勝つなどし、注目された。松岡はこのときすでに、錦織の才能を見出していたという（なお、このときに錦織に敗れた高校生は、のちにTBSでアナウンサーとなる石井大裕だ）。

　松岡が錦織に初めて会ったときの印象は、「身体的には目立つ子ではないが、コートに立つ彼は天才的」というものだった。

　「あのとき僕は彼に非常に厳しく接しました」と松岡は振り返る。しかし松岡は、錦織の技術的なことを批判することは、絶対にしなかった。すでに何か特別なものを持っていたから、彼のやり方を変えさせることでそれを失って欲しくなかったのだ。松岡は、錦織が成功する子だと分かっていたからこそ、非常に厳しく接したのだという。

　松岡はさらに、トッププレーヤーとなるためには、ただテニスがうまければいいわけではない、英語や外国の文化に触れなければだめだ、と加える。「修造チャレンジ」では実際に、テニスの練習だけでなく、子供たちに英語で自己表現をさせるトレーニングも行っている。

Kei, a Shimane native who was becoming a top-ranked player in Japan, touched on an even wider world at the age of 12. He decided to join a trial offered by an American tennis school, IMG Academy.

IMG Academy is a very prestigious tennis school based in Florida. Its predecessor is the Nick Bollettieri Tennis Academy, which was established in 1978 by a renowned famous coach Nick Bollettieri, who was inducted into the International Tennis Hall of Fame in 2014. IMG Academy has turned out famous top-ranked players such as Andre Agassi, Monica Seles and Maria Sharapova. In 1987, the International Management Group (IMG), a managing company to which some famous athletes belong, took over the Nick Bollettieri Tennis Academy, and it evolved into IMG Academy with multi-sport training facilities for golf and soccer players as well as tennis athletes.

The trial lasted three weeks in total, but Kei really enjoyed the period when he was immersed in tennis with 800 other students at IMG Academy.

■native 图〜出身の人　■prestigious 形名声のある　■predecessor 图前にあったもの
■induct into（地位などに）就かせる　■turn out 輩出する　■take over 買収する
■last 動続く　■period 图期間　■be immersed in 〜にどっぷり漬かっている

島根から全国レベルで活躍し始めた錦織は12歳のとき、さらに広い世界に触れることになる。アメリカのテニススクール「IMGアカデミー」が東京都内で行ったトライアルに参加することになったのだ。

　IMGアカデミーは、フロリダに拠点を構える名門中の名門テニススクールだ。2014年に国際テニス殿堂入りした名テニスコーチ、ニック・ボロテリーが1978年に開校したニック・ボロテリー・テニスアカデミーが前身で、これまでアンドレ・アガシやモニカ・セレシュ、マリア・シャラポワなど、世界ランキング上位の有名選手を数多く輩出している。1987年に、名だたるアスリートが所属するマネジメント会社として知られるインターナショナル・マネジメント・グループ（IMG）がニック・ボロテリー・テニスアカデミーを買収。テニスのみならずゴルフやサッカーの選手育成も含めた、マルチスポーツのトレーニング施設IMGアカデミーとして生まれ変わった。

　IMGアカデミーのトライアルは、全日程を合計すると3週間におよんだ。しかしIMGアカデミーで800人の候補生に囲まれてテニス漬けの毎日だった時間を、錦織は心から楽しんだという。

"The top players that train at IMG Academy really showed me how hard I needed to work to become a professional player," Kei says.

The head coach of IMG Academy Gabe Jaramillo immediately felt when he first saw Kei in the Tokyo trial that he had special talent. At that time, he was ranked No. 3 among Japanese junior players. But the instant he appeared on court, Jaramillo remembers he was fascinated by how perfect his footwork and racket head speed were, and how quickly and clearly he saw the openings on the court. But there was something that impressed Jaramillo more. The 12-year-old boy never seemed nervous in the presence of Morita, the founder of Masaaki Morita Tennis Fund, or famous coaches and former professional tennis players. He did not get cold feet in the setting, but found the weak spot of the opponent's court and hit a smash into it. Jaramillo was impressed—this lack of fear is the most important element for a champion.

■instant 名瞬間　■opening 名空所　■presence 名存在　■get cold feet おじけづく
■setting 名状況　■weak spot 弱点　■opponent 名対戦相手

「アカデミーで指導してくれたトップ選手たちが、プロになるためにはいかに努力が大切かを教えてくれました」と振り返る。
　IMGアカデミーのヘッドコーチ、ゲイブ・ハラミロは、東京のトライアルで初めて錦織を見たとき、特別な才能を持った子であるとすぐに感じたという。当時の錦織は、ジュニアで国内3位にランキングされていた。しかしコートに立った途端に、その足の速さ、ラケットのヘッドスピードの速さ、コートの空きを見つけるうまさに目が行ったと、ハラミロはいう。しかしこうしたことよりも、大きく印象に残ったことがあった。それは、錦織には「恐れがまったくない」ということだ。盛田ファンドの創立者である盛田や著名なコーチ陣、元プロ選手などそうそうたるメンバーが見ているのに、わずか12歳の少年がまったく物怖じしていなかった。それどころか、雰囲気に飲まれて怖気づくこともなく、相手コートの穴を見つけてはそこに打ち込んでいた。そんな錦織の姿に、ハラミロは感銘を受けたという。この恐れのなさが、チャンピオンにとってもっとも大切な要素なのだ。

Also, the short stay in the U.S.A. during the latter half of the trial showed that Kei could compete in different situations and adjust to the American lifestyle.

However, Jaramillo was aware of Kei's weak points. He judged Kei's technique as follows: "His forehand was explosive, but his volleying was poor and his service technique was that of a beginner."

03 Morita Foundation

Playing at the global level became a reality for Kei when he was selected to train at IMG Academy when he was only a junior high school student at the age of 12. His parents named him "Kei" because they really wanted him to be a world-class person. Kiyoshi and Eri had a vague hope that their son would grow up to be a citizen of the world. This is why they chose a name that could be pronounced easily by foreigners.

■latter 形後の ■be aware of ～に気づいている ■judge 動評価する ■as follows 次のとおりで ■explosive 形爆発的な ■service 名サーブ ■foundation 名基金、ファンド ■vague 形漠然とした ■citizen 名市民

さらに、トライアル過程の後半で行うアメリカでの短期留学の間に、錦織がさまざまな状況下で勝負できることや、アメリカでの生活に順応できるであろうことなども伺い知ることができたという。
　ただしハラミロは、錦織の弱点も見抜いていた。錦織の技術面に対するハラミロの評価は、「フォアハンドは爆発的。しかしボレーとサーブはまだまだ」というものだった。

錦織を育んだ盛田ファンド

　わずか12歳、中学生にして、IMGアカデミーへの留学という形で、錦織にとって「世界」が現実になりつつあった。錦織の「圭」という名前には、世界に通用する人物に育って欲しいという、両親の強い思いが込められていた。漠然とではあるが、息子には地球市民として育って欲しい、という願いが清志と恵理にはあったのだ。だからこそ、外国人にも発音しやすい名前をつけた。

When Kei was born, being global was on his parents' mind. But they could not afford to let him learn tennis abroad easily. It generally costs 7.5–8.5 million yen annually to cover the tuition fees and accommodation if one wants one's child to polish their tennis skills. That said, it was Masaaki Morita Tennis Fund (MMTF) that enabled Kei, who was highly regarded by IMG Tennis Academy, to go abroad to learn tennis.

MMTF was founded by Masaaki Morita (currently the honorary president of the Japan Tennis Association). He is a former vice president of Sony and a younger brother of Akio Morita, one of its co-founders. After he retired, he established the Foundation with his private fortune in 2000. It was authorized as an incorporated foundation in 2003.

When Morita retired from the business world, where he had always set and achieved aggressive goals, he got frustrated because he missed having targets. He could not spend his time doing nothing, he thought about it daily—he had to do something.

■afford to ～するだけの経済的余裕がある　■cover 動（費用を）負担する
■accommodation 名宿泊設備　■be highly regarded by 高く評価される　■private fortune 私財　■authorize 動 ～を認可する　■daily 副日々

錦織が生まれたときから、両親の念頭にはすでに「世界」があったことになるわけだが、だからといって無条件に海外にテニス留学をさせることができるような、経済的に恵まれた環境だったわけではなかった。子供をテニス留学させるには、一般的に学費と寮費だけで年間750万円から850万円ほどはかかるといわれている。IMGテニスアカデミーにその才能を見出された錦織が留学を実現できたのは、盛田テニスファンドのおかげだった。

　盛田テニスファンドは、ソニー創業者のひとり盛田昭夫の実弟であり、同社副社長だった盛田正明（現日本テニス協会名誉会長）が、経営から退いたあと、2000年に私財を投げ打って設立した。正式に財団法人として認可されたのは2003年となる。

　盛田は、それまで常に厳しい目標を立てては達成してきたビジネスの世界から退いたとき、目標を失ってしまったことに焦った。このままではいけない、何かしなくては、と悩む日々だった。しかしあるとき、自分が目標を持つより、若い人に目標を与えて頑張ってもらいたい、という考えが生まれてきた。

Then, it occurred to him that he should encourage younger people by giving them a goal, rather than having his own goal.

This led to the idea that he should try to do what other people couldn't do in his favorite sport, tennis. Masaru Ibuka, another co-founder of Sony, always said: "You should do what other people cannot do." Morita had absorbed this philosophy.

Morita once told a foreign reporter why he had established the Foundation; an observation led him to the idea of overseas tennis training for children. He noticed that Japanese kids played a beautiful technical game at home but they couldn't win overseas. Morita thought he should try something different. This led to the idea of sending kids overseas.

Olivier van Lindonk, Kei's agent, understands Morita's clear vision, and adds:

Morita's belief that Japan was not a suitable place to breed champions was pretty controversial at that time. But now it turned out that Kei became a world-class player and proved that Morita was right. Morita looks like a hero now.

■occur to ～の心にふと浮かぶ　■rather than ～よりはむしろ　■lead to ～に至る
■absorb 動（思想などを）身につける　■observation 名所見、観察結果　■at home 自国で　■agent 名代理人　■suitable 形ふさわしい　■controversial 形議論を引き起こす

その考えは、「自分の好きなテニスで、今まで誰もやれなかったことをやってみる」という思いに至ったのだという。ソニー創業者の一人である井深大は、「他人にやれないことをやれ」と常に口にしていた。盛田にもこの哲学がすっかり身についていたのだ。

　盛田はファンドを設立した理由を、海外メディアに語ったことがあった。ある気づきが、子供たちに海外でテニスのトレーニングを受けさせるという考えに至ったのだという。それは、日本の子供たちが、国内の大会では技術的に非常に優れた試合をするのに、海外ではなぜかまったく勝てないということだ。盛田は、今までとは何か違うことを試してみる必要があると感じた。この気づきが、子供たちを海外へ送り出すというアイデアにつながったという。

　現在、錦織のマネージャーを務めるオリビエ・ヴァン・リンドンクはこうした盛田の明確な狙いを理解した上で、次のように説明を加える。

　日本がチャンピオンを育てる場所としてふさわしくないという盛田の信念は、当時、議論を醸し出したという。しかし、錦織が世界レベルで活躍し、盛田の考え方が正しかったことを証明してくれた。おかげで、盛田は今やまるでヒーローのような存在だという。

He further states that Japanese culture—with its harmony and rigidly hierarchical social structures—does not help individual success.

Respect is a huge part of Japanese culture. But according to van Lindonk, that does not work on the court. It is a competition out there. For example, if you put a young player on the court with an older pro, and the young player gets his ball in but the older player says it is out, he will not challenge it. So with these kids, IMG Academy had to break them down and then build them up again.

The aim of the Foundation is to find talented tennis players in their childhood, let them get training abroad and develop them into world-leading players in the future. But the founder Morita had played tennis just as a hobby. He had played tennis for a long time, but never taken a formal lesson. So he asked friends from his tennis circle to help establish the Foundation. When he explained the Foundation project to Mark McCormack, one of his best friends and the founder of IMG, McCormack told him about the Nick Bollettieri Tennis Academy, which IMG

■rigidly 副 厳格に　■hierarchical 形 階層的な　■out there あちらでは　■in 名（判定の）イン　■out 名（判定の）アウト　■challenge 動 異議申し立てをする　■break ~ down ~を取り壊す　■build ~ up ~を組み立てる

リンドンクはさらに、調和や厳しい上下関係を重視する日本の文化は、個人が成功を収める助けにはならないと続ける。

　日本の文化では、尊敬が非常に重んじられている。しかしリンドンクが言うには、コート上にまでこの尊敬の思いを持ち込んでしまっては、だめなのだ。なぜなら、コートは戦いの場だからだ。例えば、若い選手を、年上のプロ選手とコートに立たせるとしよう。若い選手がボールをライン内に入れたとしても、もし年上の選手が今のショットはアウトだったと言えば、若い選手はそれにチャレンジすることさえしない。強い選手を育てるために、IMGアカデミーでは日本のこうした子供たちの考え方をいったんリセットしてから、組み立て直すという作業をしなければならないのだという。

　ファンドは、テニスの才能を持った選手を子供のうちに見出し、海外にテニス留学させ、将来的に世界のトップを狙えるような選手に育てることを目指している。そんなファンドを設立した盛田だが、彼自身はこれまで、趣味の延長としてしかプレーしかことがなかった。テニス歴は長いものの、正式にテニスのレッスンを受けたことすらなかったのだ。そこで、テニス界の知人の協力を得ながら、ファンドを形にしていくこととなった。親友のIMG創業者マーク・マコーマックにファンドの構想を説明すると、当時IMGが買収したばかりのニック・ボ

had just acquired. Morita and McCormack went to Florida to talk face-to-face with Bollettieri. The negotiation was a success; Bollettieri agreed to accept young players from MMTF.

One must pass three stages of a selection process to obtain a scholarship from MMTF to study abroad. In the first stage, the Foundation chooses candidate players (currently it accepts open applications). Then in the second stage, the Foundation invites the head coach of IMG Academy from the U.S.A. to Tokyo and offers a trial to the players who have passed the first stage. Those who pass the second stage go to Florida for the third stage, a two-week training at IMG Academy. There, four children from different countries share a room. Children with the same nationality are not allowed to stay in the same room. In this way, they see if the candidates can adapt to life in the U.S.A. and the dormitory life in IMG Academy on top of assessing their tennis skills. IMG Academy gives feedback to MMTF, which in turn asks the players and their parents whether they are willing to get training at IMG Academy for at least

■acquire 動 買収する　■open application 公募　■trial 名 選考会　■see if 〜かどうかを確かめる　■adapt to 〜に順応する　■assess 動 査定する　■at least 最低でも

ロテリー・テニスアカデミーを紹介してくれた。盛田とマコーマックは、フロリダまで直接出向いてボロテリーと交渉し、選手を受け入れてもらえることになった。

　盛田ファンドがサポートする海外留学の奨学選手として選ばれるには、3次まである選考過程を突破しなくてはならない。まずは1次選考として、ファンド側が選手を選ぶ（現在は公募制）。続く2次選考では、IMGアカデミーのヘッドコーチをアメリカから都内に招き、1次で選出した選手を集めて選考会を行う。2次選考を通過した選手は、実際にフロリダへ行ってIMGアカデミーで2週間のトレーニングを受ける。これが3次選考だ。ここでは、国籍の違う子供たち4人が1部屋に割り振られて寝泊まりをすることになる。同じ国籍の子供は意図的に、同じ部屋にはしないのだという。こうして、テニスの実力のみならず、アメリカでの生活やアカデミーでの寮生活に順応できるか否かが判断される。ここでの結果をIMGアカデミーからフィードバックしてもらい、選手と家族に対し、もし奨学選手として選ばれたら、最低1年間はIMGアカデミーでトレーニングを受ける覚悟はあるかという意思を確認する。選手も家族もこれに承諾した場合、晴れて合格となる。

one year if they are chosen as a scholarship player. If both the players and their families accept the condition, they pass selection.

A scholarship player gets training for one year, from September to May. During training, the Foundation provides all the funds necessary for the students to pay for travel expenses to and from the U.S.A., lesson fees, accommodation, tuition at local schools, tuition for Japanese distance learning (if any), tour costs if they join a tour, and so on. Specific goals are given to each player in accordance with their level, and if they meet the goals by the end of May, the training period as a scholarship player is extended by one year. They can get training at IMG Academy up until they are 18 years old and no longer are a junior player. But if they fail to meet the goals, then the training is terminated. This may sound severe, but it makes sense because the Foundation has the ultimate aim of developing a world-class player. Many players have failed to achieve the targets for extension of the training period, and have returned to Japan.

■condition 图条件 ■fund 图資金 ■if any もしあるなら ■and so on ～など ■in accordance with ～に従って ■meet a goal 目標を達成する ■terminate 動打ち切る ■sound 動 ～に思われる

このような選考を経て奨学選手になると、9月から翌年5月までを1年として留学することになる。留学中は、アメリカへの渡航費をはじめ、IMGアカデミーのレッスン料、宿泊費、現地学校の学費、日本の通信教育を受ける場合はその学費、さらにツアーに参加する際の遠征費用などが支給される。各選手には5月末までに達成すべき目標がレベルに応じて与えられ、これを満たすことができれば、奨学選手としての留学が1年間延長される。最長で、18歳のジュニア卒業まで留学することができる。この目標をクリアできない場合、留学はそこで打ち切りとなる。この厳しさは当然、世界レベルで活躍できるトッププレーヤーを育てるという、高い目標をファンドが掲げているからだ。しかしこれまで多くの選手が、留学続行のための目標を達成することができず、帰国していった。

Kei passed the above-mentioned selection process and was chosen as a fourth-generation scholarship player in 2003 and went to Florida with three other players. This was when he was 13. Kei kept achieving the targets and was able to get training in the U.S.A. as a scholarship player until he made his pro debut in 2007 when he was 17 years and 10 months old. He became the first player who "graduated" from IMG Academy without being kicked out halfway. By 2014, MMTF had sent 17 players to IMG Academy, but only two of them, Kei and Yoshito Nishioka, were able to receive support until they completed their career as a junior player.

■above-mentioned 形先に述べた　■make one's debut デビューを果たす　■kick out 退学させる　■halfway 副途中で

錦織はこの選考過程を経て2003年、盛田ファンド第4期の奨学選手として選ばれ、他3名とともにフロリダに渡った。13歳のときだった。錦織は与えられた目標を毎年達成し続け、2007年に17歳10カ月でプロデビューを果たすまで、奨学生として留学を続けることができた。留学を打ち切られることなく、無事「卒業」できた最初の選手となったのだ。2014年時点で、これまで盛田ファンドが送り出した17人のうち、ジュニア卒業までファンドの援助を受け続けることができたのは、錦織と西岡良仁の2人だけである。

覚えておきたい英語表現

Kei became familiar with tennis and really **got into** it.
（p.12, 10行目）
錦織はテニスに親しみ、テニスにのめり込んでいった。

【用語】　get into〜：夢中になる、のめり込む、はまっている
　　　　be into〜：熱中している、はまっている

【解説】その対象そのものの中に入るほど好き、つまり「熱中している、はまっている」という意味になります。getを使わず、be into〜を使っても同じような意味です。何か自分が好きなことを話したいときや趣味について尋ねられたときに使える表現です。他にもMy favorite (sport/food/book) is 〜．と言っても良いですが、I am into〜．やI get into〜．を使うとより英語的な表現になります。

【例文】　Q：What do you do for fun?
　　　　　　ご趣味は何ですか？
　　　　A：I'm really into cooking, so I often cook dinner for my family.
　　　　　　料理にかなりはまっています。それでよく家族に夕食を作るんですよ。

I've gotten into baseball since I was a junior high school student. I can't wait for watching World Baseball Classic (WBC) games this year.
中学生になってから、野球に熱中しています。今年の世界野球選手権の試合を観るのが待ち遠しいです。

> The result of the game was entirely **up to** him. (p.16, 5行目)
> 試合結果は完全に自分次第だった。

【用語】 be up to~：~次第です、~に任せる

【解説】be up to~を英英辞典で調べるとto be one's responsibilityと出てきます。つまり「その人の責任である＝その人次第である、その人に任せる」という訳になります。例えばIt's up to you.で「あなた次第です」という意味になり、口語ではUp to you.とも言います。相手の人に決断を委ねたり、その人次第であると言いたいときに使うことができる表現です。しかし海外ではbe up to~を使いすぎると自分で物事を決めることができない優柔不断(indecisive)な人としてあまり良い印象をもたれないので、気をつけましょう。

【例文】 I don't mind which restaurant we'll go to. It's up to you.
どのレストランでも問題ないよ。きみにお任せします。

Whether the project will be successful is up to him.
その事業が成功するかどうかは彼次第だ。

> He did not **get cold feet** in the setting. (p.24, 下から5行目)
> 彼は雰囲気（状況）におじけづかなかった。

【用語】 get cold feet：おじけづく

【解説】get cold feetで「おじけづく」という意味のinformalな（口語的な）表現になります。何か躊躇したり、ためらうときに使います。しかし英語を母語としない私たち日本人にとっては、なかなか出てこない表現ですね。音読や暗唱を通してこの表現をマスターしましょう。

【例文】 My brother began getting cold feet as his wedding day approached.
結婚式が近づくにつれて、兄はおじけづき始めました。

Morita's belief that Japan was not a suitable place to breed champions was pretty **controversial**. (p.30, 下から5行目)

日本がチャンピオンを育てる場所としてふさわしくないという盛田の信念は、議論を醸し出したという。

【用語】 controversial：議論を引き起こす、賛否両論のある

【解説】controversialは「議論を引き起こす」という意味の形容詞です。英検やIELTSなどのライティングがある試験では、社会問題など社会性の高い分野の話題について自分の主張を記述することが求められます。その際このワードを「導入」の一部として使うと、それ以降スムーズに自分の主張に進むことができます。例えばp.32, 1-3行目のセンテンスを自分の主張としたとき、以下のようにすると良いでしょう。

【例文】 It has been a *controversial* issue about whether Japan is a suitable place to breed champions in the field of tennis or not. In my opinion, Japanese culture—with its harmony and rigidly hierarchical social structures—does not help individual success.

日本がテニスの分野でチャンピオンを育成するのに適した国かどうかは、議論の余地がある問題です。私は、調和や厳しい上下関係を重視する日本の文化は、個人が成功を収める助けにはならないと考えます。

このように最初の文で、その問題（ここでは日本がトップ選手の育成環境に適しているかどうかについて議論の余地がある）の社会的背景について説明し、その次の文で自分の主張を書くという流れです。

Chapter 2
Anguish

*Plagued by Injuries
(2003–2010)*

第2章
「苦悩」

米国留学〜ケガで苦しんだ
時期（2003〜2010）

Kei began his new life in the East Coast state of Florida, 12,000 km away from his hometown. He was only a 13-year-old eighth grader. The shift from easygoing Matsue, Shimane to the tennis mecca in Florida, far away from his parents, was enormous. Also, Kei couldn't speak English at all then. Though he had been studying English since he was a child, his English was never good enough to live in the U.S.A. But he didn't hesitate, as he later recalls: "I thought I wanted to go to Florida at once. I can do anything for tennis."

The founder Nick Bollettieri, now 83, still coaches younger players. He understands Kei and appreciates his talents. So he often appears in the foreign media as a commentator on Nishikori. In his book "Changing the Game," he praises Kei: "I have seen thousands of tennis players over the past 60 years and can identify only three who have had the gift of magic hands." They were Xavier Malisse (Best ATP

■state 名（アメリカの）州　■shift from ~ to　～から…への変化　■easygoing 形のんびりした　■mecca 名メッカ、中心地　■not ~ at all まったくもって～ない　■though 接～にもかかわらず　■at once すぐに　■praise 動 ~を賞賛する　■identify 動（存在を）発見する

こうして、錦織は故郷から1万2千キロメートル離れたアメリカ東海岸のフロリダ州で新しい生活を始めることとなった。若干13歳、中学2年生。のんびりとした島根県松江市から、親元を遠く離れたフロリダにあるテニスのメッカへの移住という、あまりにも大きすぎる変化を迎えることになったのだ。しかも当時、錦織は英語をまったくしゃべることができなかった。子供のころから英語を学んだとはいえ、実際にアメリカで生活するだけの英語力はなかったのだ。しかし、「フロリダに行きたい、ってすぐに思いました。テニスのためなら何でもする」とのちに語ったように、錦織に迷いはなかった。

　創設者のニック・ボロテリーは、83歳にして今も現役で選手を指導している。海外メディアの記事に、錦織を語る人物として頻繁に登場するほど、錦織をよく理解しており、錦織の才能を買っている存在だ。その著書『Changing the Game』の中でも、「60年以上にわたり何千、何万というテニス選手を見てきたが、魔法の手とも言える天性に恵まれた選手はわずか3人。グザビエ・マリス（自己最高世界ランキング19位）、マルセロ・リオス（同1位）、そして錦織圭だ」と、錦織を賞賛している。

ranking: no. 19), Marcelo Rios (Best ATP ranking: no. 1), and Kei Nishikori.

"I Want to Be Number One in the World"

When Kei got to the Academy, Bollettieri wrote that his impression of Nishikori as a player was that "his limbs [were] no weaker than any other players." But on his arrival in Florida, he was just a boy, scared to death. Bollettieri was worried that he might soon go back to Japan because he missed his family.

Because of the language problem, Bollettieri said that Kei just wouldn't talk. He was very stoic. He never smiled. He missed his parents and he missed his food.

Kei was calm and scared off court. But Bollettieri found that he was extremely quick and made strong shots on court. It didn't take Bollettieri very long to realize that he had extraordinary talent.

■get to 〜に到着する ■limb 名手足 ■scared to death 死ぬほど怖がっている
■miss 動 〜が恋しい ■stoic 形感情を表に出さない ■off court コートの外では
■extraordinary 形ただならぬ

「I want to be number one in the world」

　錦織がアカデミーに到着した当初、ボロテリーが記録に記した錦織の選手としての印象は、「手足の強さはどのテニス選手にも劣らない」というものだった。しかしフロリダに到着したばかりの錦織は、死ぬほど怖がって怯えた少年だった。ホームシックですぐに日本に帰ってしまうのではないかと、ボロテリーは心配したという。

　ボロテリーいわく、英語がまったくしゃべれないという言葉の壁から、錦織は口を開こうとしなかった。非常にストイックで、笑顔を見せるなどということもなかった。両親や日本食を恋しがっている様子だったという。

　しかしボロテリーは、コート外ではおとなしく怯えていた錦織が、ひとたびコートに立つと俊敏に動き回り、腕の強さを見せつけることに気づいた。それがただならぬ才能を持った選手であることが分かるまでに、時間はかからなかった。

"He was such a shy, quiet kid. He couldn't communicate with anyone. It was super tough," says van Lindonk, looking back on the time when Kei had just arrived at Florida.

The coach of IMG Academy Jaramillo says he found it very difficult to get Kei to open up initially. Kei didn't have any confidence, his manner was withdrawn and he didn't give coaches much feedback. But after a while, the instructors got to know that Kei liked straightforward coaching techniques. So for the first couple of years they kept to a tight schedule and set to work on Kei's service and throwing motion. Kei threw hundreds of American footballs and baseballs in order to develop the basics.

Also, Jaramillo reveals that Kei could hardly speak a word of English, but there was one thing he could clearly say: "I want to be number one in the world."

■tough 形辛い ■look back on （過去を）振り返る ■open up 心を開く ■withdrawn 形内にこもった ■get to know ～を知るようになる ■throwing 图手で物を投げること ■in order to ～するために ■reveal 動（情報などを）明かす ■can hardly ほとんど～できない

リンドンクは、錦織がフロリダに到着したばかりのころを振り返り、「シャイで物静かな子でした。誰ともコミュニケーションできず、（彼にとっては）非常に辛い状況でした」と話す。

　ハラミロによると、IMGアカデミーのコーチ陣は当初、錦織の心を開くのに苦労したらしい。錦織はまったく自信がなく控えめで、アカデミーに自分の意見を伝えることをあまりしなかった。しかししばらくすると、錦織が分かりやすい単刀直入なコーチング・スタイルが好きだということが、指導陣に分かってきた。そのためアカデミーは、最初の1～2年はとにかくスケジュールを詰め込み、サーブとサーブトスの改善に取り組んだ。基礎を叩き込むために、アメリカンフットボールや野球のボールを使ったサーブトス練習を何百回も繰り返したという。

　またハラミロは当時の錦織が、英語はしゃべれなかったものの、1つだけ英語できちんと言えたことがあった、と明かす。「I want to be number one in the world.」（世界で1位になりたい）はっきりと英語でそう言ったのだ。

Kei himself recalls, "Even though I couldn't speak a word of English, I didn't feel homesick." He was too busy developing his technique. He was blessed with a powerful forehand but was aware that he had to work on his service motion and footwork around the court.

"For the first couple of years it was really tough to communicate with my coaches and my friends because I couldn't speak the language," Kei says. But he was very happy just to play tennis all day.

Life in the Academy was just immersion in tennis. The students practiced tennis in the morning, followed by three hours of school lessons—two hours of which were devoted to learning English—and more tennis in the afternoon.

According to Jaramillo, as the Academy didn't have any Japanese coaches or translators, it hired someone who Kei already knew for the first couple of years to ensure that his transition was trouble free. The Academy also enrolled him at a school where they taught English as a second language.

■even though 〜ではあるけれども　■be blessed with 〜に恵まれている
■immersion 图浸すこと　■followed by その後に〜が続く　■ensure 動〜を保証する
■trouble free 問題なく　■enroll 動入学させる

錦織本人は当時を振り返り、英語は全然しゃべれなかったが、ホームシックにはならなかったと語っている。自分の技術を磨くのに懸命だったのだ。パワフルなフォアハンドに恵まれてはいたものの、サーブとフットワークをもっと上達させる必要がある、と自覚していたという。

　最初の数年は、英語がしゃべれなかったためコーチや友達とコミュニケーションを取るのが非常に難しかったと、錦織は言う。しかし、1日中テニスができることが、ただ幸せだった。

　アカデミーでの生活は、まさにテニス漬けだった。生徒たちは午前中にテニスを練習し、その後3時間、学校の授業を行う。うち2時間は英語の時間にあてられた。午後、さらにテニスの練習を行った。

　ハラミロによると、アカデミーには日本人のコーチや通訳がいなかったため、最初の数年は錦織がすでに知っている人物を日本から採用し、錦織のアメリカへの移住が問題なくスムーズに行くように努めた。さらに、英語を第二言語として教えてくれる学校に錦織を入学させたのだった。

As a result, Kei attended a local school in Florida, had additional English lessons, and took long-distance learning courses in the Japanese curriculum. All these should have been extra burdens. But Jaramillo understood that Kei was clearly different from other students. IMG Academy have accepted tens of thousands of talented children, but Jaramillo says that very few children work hard to unfold their potential.

But Kei was never like that. If Jaramillo asked him to turn up at 7 a.m. for a training session on court, he would be there at 6:45 a.m. checking his rackets and shoes. That way they were hitting balls just at 7 a.m.

■as a result 結果的に　■extra 形余分の　■burden 名負荷　■unfold 動開花する
■turn up 現れる

錦織はこうして、フロリダの現地校に通いつつ英語の授業も受け、さらに通信制で日本の学校教育も受けていた。そのため、テニス以外の負担も大きかっただろう。しかしハラミロは、錦織が明らかに他の生徒たちと違うことを理解していた。IMGアカデミーはその歴史のなかで、何万人という才能溢れる子供たちを受け入れてきた。しかし、持てる潜在能力を花開かせるほど努力をする子供は非常に少ない、とハラミロは言う。

　しかし錦織は、最初からまったく違っていたのだ。ハラミロが、コートでトレーニングを行うから朝7時に集合するように、と伝えると、錦織は6時45分にはコートに来ていた。そして時間になるまで、ラケットやシューズの調整をしているのだ。おかげで、7時ちょうどにボールを打ち始めることができたのだった。

A "Dream Player" with Talent

As soon as he started a new life in Florida in 2003, Kei began to stand out. He was placed in the Top 4 at the Eddie Herr International Junior Championships in December. In the same month, he took second place at the Junior Orange Bowl International Tennis Championship (U-14 singles). The Junior Orange Bowl is a Grade A tournament like Grand Slams.

For Jaramillo, Kei was a "dream player for a coach." With his immense talent, Kei already had the presence of a champion. After working with numerous top players like Andre Agassi and Pete Sampras for many years, Jaramillo is convinced that talent is everything.

Working with talented players requires very organized practice sessions and a lot of energy from the coaches. And Kei was also a special player who always forced them to work hard, Jaramillo says. He spent thousands of hours correcting errors and improving skills, filled with a sense of commitment.

■stand out 頭角をあらわす ■take second place 準優勝する ■immense 形非常に大きな ■presence 图風格 ■convinced 形確信して ■force someone to （人に）〜せざるを得ないようにする ■correct 動修正する ■filled with a sense of commitment 責任感でいっぱいである

才能あふれる「夢の選手」

　こうして、フロリダでの生活を始めた2003年、錦織はさっそく頭角をあらわし始めた。12月に行われたジュニアの登竜門エディ・ハー・ジュニア選手権でベスト4に進出。同じく12月のジュニア・オレンジボウル国際選手権（男子14歳以下シングルス）では準優勝した。このオレンジボウルは、グランドスラム同様、グレードAの大会だ。

　ハラミロからみた錦織は、「コーチにとって夢の選手」だった。才能に溢れ、チャンピオンの風格をすでに持っていた。それまで、アンドレ・アガシやピート・サンプラスなど、数え切れないほどのトップ選手を育ててきたハラミロは、「才能がすべて」と言い切る。

　しかし才能のある選手を育てるには、選手に組織だった練習をさせ、エネルギーを注ぐなど、コーチの方もさらなる努力が求められる。そしてコーチ陣が常に努力をせざるを得ないほど、錦織は優れた選手だと、ハラミロは言う。エラーをしたらそれを正して技術を向上させる。このようなことに、黙々と長い時間を費やすストイックさを持ち合わせているのだ。他の誰

He understood that he didn't have to prove anything to anybody. He just simply went about his business and worked hard. Jaramillo says in his blog that Kei is not only talented, but also spares no effort.

Because Kei was special, the Academy treated him differently. His training was very individualized, and the coaches showed Kei how much they believed in him during practice.

According to Jaramillo, Kei spent a lot of time training on the clay courts until he was 15 years old. From 15 to 17, Kei's goal was to obtain a Top 10 International Tennis Federation (ITF) junior world ranking. During this period, he was training four hours daily on court plus two hours off court. In contrast to the small, thin boy when he had just arrived at the U.S.A., Kei was now getting very strong, and his shoulders and lower body were incredibly well built. His speed also improved dramatically.

■go about one's business 自分のすべきことをする ■blog 图ブログ ■spare 動~を出し惜しむ ■treat 動待遇する ■individualized 形個人に合わせた ■clay court クレーコート《粘土や赤土の上に砂をまいたコート》 ■federation 图連盟 ■in contrast to ~とは大違いで

かに自分の力を証明してみせる必要性など感じずに、ただ自分のやるべきことをこなし、努力を重ねる。ハラミロは、錦織が才能だけに頼らず、努力を怠らない選手であると、そのブログで語っている。

　錦織は特別な才能を持った特別な選手であったため、アカデミー側も特別に対応した。錦織に合わせたトレーニングが組まれ、練習中も、コーチ陣がどれほど錦織を信頼しているかを、本人にきちんと伝えるよう務めたという。

　ハラミロによると、錦織が15歳までの時期は、クレーコートでの練習に長い時間を割いた。15歳から17歳の時期には、錦織はITF（国際テニス連盟）ジュニアランキングで上位10位に入ることを目標にしていた。このころは、コートで4時間、コート外で2時間、計6時間を毎日トレーニングで費やしていた。おかげで、アメリカに移ったばかりのころは小さくてきゃしゃな少年だった錦織だったが、このころまでにはすっかり、その足腰や肩は鍛えられていた。そしてスピードも劇的に向上した。

07 Breaking out of His Shell to Become a Leading Player

When Kei came to the U.S.A., Toru Yonezawa was his first coach. Yonezawa spent a great deal of time with Kei in developing technique. But Jaramillo felt it necessary to make a change because Yonezawa only allowed Kei to play with other Japanese players from MMFT. He thought Kei should take advantage of the other good players they had at the Academy. So Jaramillo decided to change Kei's personal coach. He replaced Yonezawa with Cesar Castaneda, a coach from Peru who was very familiar with the ITF Junior Circuit.

Kei had been kind of protected by Yonezawa a lot, but he gradually came out of his shell after this change.

■shell 图殻　■great deal of 多くの　■take advantage of ～の利点を活用する
■replace 動 ～を交代させる　■kind of ～のようなたぐいの

殻を破ってアカデミーの中心へ

　アメリカに移った当初、錦織には米沢徹がコーチについていた。米沢は、錦織と二人三脚で練習に取り組み、基礎的な技術を叩き込んだ。しかしハラミロは、米沢が錦織を盛田ファンドから送られてきた日本人選手とばかり練習させる現状を変える必要性を感じた。アカデミーには優秀な選手が世界中から集まっているという利点を生かし、他の選手たちとも練習させるべきだと考えたのだ。そこでハラミロは、パーソナルコーチを変える決断をする。米沢に変わって錦織を指導することになったのは、ITFジュニアサーキットに詳しいペルー出身のセザール・カスタネーダだった。

　それまでは、米沢に大切に守られてきたかのような錦織だったが、このころから徐々に殻を破るようになる。

At first, Kei couldn't speak English, lacked confidence, and was shorter and slighter than other students at the Academy. But a certain event gave him self-confidence. Jaramillo made Kei play a challenge match against Philip Bester one evening. Bester was a Canadian and one of the best junior players in the world among the players at IMG Academy. Before then, Kei had played in obscurity against other Japanese players on the back courts of the Academy. But this challenge match was played in front of the entire Academy. It was advertised on every available door, lamp post and notice board, encouraging all of the students to come and watch.

Jaramillo recalls that Kei wasn't keen on the match. The opponent was one year older and much taller. It's true that Kei had defeated a high school student in the Shuzo Challenge when he was an elementary school student. But this time, he was going to play against a top junior player in the Academy, which is full of elite players from all over the world. Things were totally different this time. Jaramillo recalls that Kei didn't believe he belonged on the same court

■short 形 小柄な ■slight 形 きゃしゃな ■in obscurity ひっそりと ■available 形 空きがあって利用できる ■notice board 掲示板 ■keen on ～に乗り気である ■elite 形 えり抜きの

英語もしゃべれず、自信もない、体格も他のアカデミー生と比べて小柄できゃしゃな中学生の錦織が、自分に自信を持てるようになった出来事があった。ハラミロが、IMGアカデミー在籍のジュニアの中でも世界のトップ選手だったカナダ出身のフィリップ・ベスターと、一晩限りのチャレンジマッチをするよう錦織に指示したのだ。それまでは、アカデミーの奥にあるコートでひっそりと、日本人同士で練習していた錦織だった。しかしこのチャレンジマッチは、アカデミーのみんなが見ているなかで行われることになった。試合に先立ち、アカデミー内のドア、柱、掲示板、ありとあらゆるところにポスターを貼って試合が告知されていたのだ。

　ハラミロによると、錦織はこの試合に乗り気ではなかったようだった。相手は1つ年上で、背も高い。もちろんかつては、修造チャレンジで小学生のときに年上の高校生を負かした経験のある錦織だ。だが今回の相手は、世界の精鋭選手が集まるアカデミーのなかでもトップのジュニア選手だ。あのときとはわけが違う。錦織は、自分がベスターと同じコートに立てるような選手ではないと感じていたようだったと、ハラミロは分析する。しかし、このチャレンジマッチを企画した時点で、錦織には互角に戦える実力がすでに備わっていたことを、ハラミロは

with players at the level of Bester. But when Jaramillo arranged the match, he knew that Kei was ready and as good as Bester. The match began at 6 p.m. The court was packed with other students who had seen the posters and come to watch the challenge match.

Kei won the match. It was a beautiful match. Jaramillo recalls that after this match Kei started to believe in himself. From that day forward, he began to practice on the top courts with the rest of the top gun students.

Success as a Junior and Senior Player

One of the goals coaches had asked him to attain was to join the French Open Junior Championship. He put this goal on a Post-It note and stuck it to his bathroom mirror so that he could read it every day.

■ready 形 用意が整って　■be packed with 〜でいっぱいである　■believe in oneself 自分に自信を持つ　■from that day forward その日以来　■rest of 他の　■top gun エリート　■attain 動 達成する　■Post-It note ポストイット付箋紙　■stick 動 貼る

わかっていた。試合開始時間は午後6時。ポスターを見て押しかけた生徒たちが見守る中、チャレンジマッチは開始となった。

　結果は、錦織が勝利を収めた。見事な試合だった。ハラミロは、この試合がきっかけとなり、錦織は自分に自信を持つようになったのではないか、と振り返る。そしてこの日以来、錦織はアカデミーの中心にあるコートで、アカデミーの他のエリート選手とともにトレーニングをするようになった。

ジュニア＆シニアでの活躍

　錦織がコーチ陣から与えられていたクリアすべき目標に、全仏オープンに出場することがあった。錦織はこの目標を付箋紙に書いて、常に目に入るよう浴室の鏡に張りつけていた。

Then in 2006, when he was 16 years old, he went to the French Open for the first time. He competed in both the singles and doubles. Unfortunately, he suffered a stomach injury, causing him to lose in the quarterfinals of the singles. But he partnered with an Argentinian Emiliano Massa to win the Junior French Open doubles title. It was the first time in both singles and doubles that a Japanese male won a Junior Grand Slam tournament. Jaramillo believes Kei would have won the singles title as well had he not suffered an injury. Kei has since said that he likes and is emotionally involved with the French Open because he won the title there when he was a junior player.

In 2006, Kei began to enter senior tournaments. He won the title at the Mexico Futures, and finished the year with the ranking, no. 603.

■singles 图シングルス《1対1の試合》　■doubles 图ダブルス《2対2の試合》
■suffer 動苦しむ　■Grand Slam グランドスラム《全豪・全仏・全米・ウィンブルドンの世界四大大会》　■since 副その後　■win the title 優勝する

そして2006年、錦織が16歳のときに初めて全仏オープンに出場することになった。ジュニアのシングルスとダブルスに出場したのだが、シングルスでは腹部の負傷に苦しみ準々決勝（ベスト8）で敗れてしまった。しかしアルゼンチン出身のエミリアノ・マサと組んだダブルスでは、優勝を飾った。グランドスラムのジュニアで日本人男子が優勝するのは、シングルス、ダブルスを通して初めてとなった。ハラミロは、「あのケガがなければ、シングルスでも優勝していただろう」としている。のちに錦織は、自分がジュニア時代に優勝した全仏オープンは好きで、思い入れがある、と語っている。

　2006年、錦織はシニアの大会にエントリーを始める。メキシコ・フューチャーズでは優勝。この年、世界ランキングを603位で終えた。

In July 2007, Kei made his debut in an ATP tournament at the Countrywide Classic (renamed the Los Angeles Open in 2012), but was defeated in the first round. The next week, he advanced to a quarterfinal at the Indianapolis Tennis Championships (now named the Atlanta Tennis Championships).

In October 2007, when he was 17 years old, he announced he was going pro. Masaaki Morita, the president of MMTF, also appeared at the press interview held in Ariake, Tokyo. Kei said there that his icon was Roger Federer and his weapon, or the main scorer, was his forehand. Morita said Kei had grown up because IMG had taken full care of him and he had had enough mental strength and adaptability to go through training for five years away from his family, let alone make his own intensive efforts. Morita added that the only anxiety, if any, would be injury.

■classic 图 伝統試合　■round 图 一試合　■press interview 記者会見　■icon 图 憧れの対象　■scorer 图 得点をあげる人（手段）　■take full care of 〜を全力で世話する　■adaptability 图 適応力　■go through （困難などを）通り抜ける

2007年7月、錦織はカントリーワイド・クラシック（ロサンゼルス・オープンとも呼ばれた大会。2012年で終了）でATPデビューを果たすが、初戦敗退となった。その翌週、インディアナ・ポリス選手権（現アトランタ・テニス選手権）では準々決勝まで勝ち抜いた。

　10月、17歳のときにプロに転向することを発表。このとき有明で行われた記者会見には盛田ファンド会長の盛田も同席した。ここで、錦織は憧れの選手をロジャー・フェデラーと言い、自分の武器は、もっとも点が取れるフォアハンドだと語った。盛田は錦織の成長について、錦織自身の努力もさることながら、IMGが錦織に力を注いだことや、5年間もひとりで外国でのトレーニングに耐えられるメンタルの強さと適応力の高さが理由だとした。このとき、今後の心配事があるとすればケガだ、と語った。

In the same month, Kei played at the Japan Open Tennis Championships making his pro debut, but lost in the first round. But at the end of 2007, his world ranking rose to no. 286.

In December 2007, Glenn Weiner replaced Rodrigo Valleho as Kei's coach. Glenn Weiner had been one of Jaramillo's students. Kei says his goal was "to break into the Top 100 and defeat some Challengers."

In January 2008, when Kei lost in an ATP Challenger circuit event at Dallas, he said his confidence was shot. So he wanted to compete at a lower-level Futures tournament. But the coaches urged him to go to the Delray Beach Open, an ATP World Tour 250 series tournament. Both Kei and the Japanese tennis world have kept this Delray Beach match in their memory and in the record books.

Kei ventured into the tournament with nothing to lose. He won one victory after another against higher ranked players, and in the final, he met world no. 12 James Blake on the court. Kei lost the first set but then won two sets, defeating Blake to win his first victory in the Tour.

■break into 入り込む　■Challenger 图チャレンジャー《世界男子テニスツアー下部の大会》　■shot 图ボロボロの　■urge someone to（人に）〜するよう強く勧める　■keep 〜 in one's memory 〜を忘れずにいる　■venture into 〜に挑む　■on 〜 after another 〜の連続で　■set 图セット《得点の単位。6ゲーム先取で1セット獲得》

その10月、錦織はジャパン・オープンに出場しプロデビューを果たすが、1回戦で敗退。しかし2007年末時点で錦織の世界ランキングは286位まで浮上した。

　2007年12月、コーチはそれまでのロドリゴ・バジェホから、ハラミロのかつての教え子であるグレン・ワイナーに交代した。錦織は2008年の目標を、「トップ100位までに入ることと、チャレンジャーで勝つこと」としていた。
　2008年1月、ダラスのチャレンジャー戦で予選敗退した錦織は、「自信はボロボロだった」（錦織談）。そのため、下位トーナメントのフューチャーズに出場したいと考えていた。しかしコーチ陣は、ATPワールド・ツアー250シリーズのデルレイビーチ国際テニス選手権で戦うよう強く勧めた。その結果、このときのデルレイビーチの大会は、錦織にとっても、日本テニス界にとっても、記憶にも記録にも残るものとなった。

　錦織は、何も失うものはない、という思いでこの大会に挑んだ。世界ランキングで自分より格上の選手を次々と打ち負かし、決勝では第1シード、世界ランキング12位（当時）のジェームズ・ブレークと当たった。1セット先取されたものの、フルセットでブレークを退け、ツアー初優勝を手に入れたのだった。

Kei was the first Japanese male player to win an ATP title since Matsuoka defeated Todd Woodbridge (Australia) in 1992. Also, at 18 years, one month and 19 days old, Kei became the second youngest player to win an ATP title after Lleyton Hewitt who won in 1998 when he was 16 years, 10 months and 18 days old. Kei improved 113 places to no. 131 in the ATP rankings.

Matsuoka said to the foreign media that he "was taken by surprise" when Kei won at Delray Beach. Matsuoka admitted Kei was mentally strong and had a great sense of dominating the play, but pointed out that players in Japan didn't physically develop as fast as other players, and that Kei was injured a lot as a junior. So he had thought maybe he would win his first title aged 20, 21 or 22.

But Kei upset Matsuoka's expectation in a good way and followed in the footsteps of Matsuoka in the Japanese male tennis world.

■be taken by surprise 不意をつかれる　■admit 動 〜を認める　■dominate 動 〜を支配する　■point out 〜を指摘する　■upset 動（予想などを）くつがえす　■footstep 図 足跡

日本人男子がATPツアーでタイトルを獲得するのは、1992年に松岡修造がトッド・ウッドブリッジ（オーストラリア）で優勝して以来だった。また、この時点で18歳1カ月19日だった錦織は、1998年に16歳10カ月18日でATPツアー制覇を飾ったレイトン・ヒューイットに次ぐ若さでのツアー優勝となった。世界ランキングは一気に113ランクを上げて、131位にまで浮上した。

　松岡はこのとき海外メディアに対して、錦織の優勝を「意外だった」と語っている。メンタルの強さやゲーム運びの良さを認めはしたものの、日本の選手は海外の選手と比べ身体的に発達が遅いため、錦織もジュニア時代にケガが多かったことを指摘。そのため、身体が出来上がる20歳から22歳くらいまでツアー優勝は無理なのではないかと予測していたのというのだ。

　しかしそんな松岡の思いを良い意味で裏切り、日本男子テニス界に、松岡に続く足跡を残すことになった。

In September, Kei became the first Japanese player to reach the U.S. Open fourth round since 1937. In the third round, he played against David Ferrer (Spain), who was ranked no. 4. Kei won a close match in five sets, with the last set at 7–5, to advance to the fourth round.

As a result, Kei broke into the Top 100 ranking for the first time, which was his initial goal as a professional, when he was ranked no. 84. Then, in October, he reached the semifinals at the Stockholm Open and his ranking advanced to no. 77. But he got a knee injury at the tournament. It wasn't serious, but it ended his season. Yet, by the end of 2008, his world ranking had risen by more than 200 places during the year to no. 63.

■play against ～を相手にする　■close match 接戦　■initial 形 最初の　■knee 名 膝
■yet 腰 けれども

このあと8月、全米オープンでは、1937年以来日本人男子初となる4回戦まで駒を進めた。しかも3回戦目で当たったのは、当時世界ランキング4位だった強豪のダビド・フェレール（スペイン）だ。フルセット、しかも最終セットは7-5という接戦の末に下したうえでの4回戦進出だった。

　世界ランキングも、錦織にとってプロ最初の目標であった100位をこのとき初めて上回り、84位となった。さらに10月、スウェーデンで行われたストックホルム・オープンで準決勝まで進み、77位に前進。しかし、大会中に膝の負傷が出てしまった。深刻なケガではないということだったが、これが錦織にとってこのシーズンの終わりを告げるものとなった。しかし世界ランキングは、1年間で200ランク以上上昇して2008年末時点で63位となった。当時18歳だった錦織は、当時上位100位内にいた選手のなかで最年少だった。

Kei, aged 18, was the youngest player in the Top 100. In IMG Academy, Kei's team was named "Project 45." This name implied the goal of breaking Shuzo Matsuoka's career-high ranking of no. 46, which was also the highest ranking of a Japanese male tennis player. This was the goal that Kei, the coaches of IMG Academy, MMTF and the Japanese tennis world had all shared since Matsuoka retired.

The long-sought world no. 45 ranking was just in front of his nose. Bollettieri gave the thumbs up to Kei's athleticism and footwork, great racket head speed, good anticipation, court sense, natural depth, and never being afraid to hit the ball, and declared that the most important thing for him now was to stay injury free. Should Kei enjoy good health, Project 45 would quickly change into Project 10. Everyone believed this would be so. But what was waiting ahead of Kei was a long, hard season plagued with injuries.

■imply 動 ～という意味を含む ■long-sought 形 念願の ■in front of one's nose 目の前に ■give thumbs up to ～にOKを出す ■anticipation 名 予測 ■depth 名（視野などの）広さ ■stay injury free 怪我のない状態を維持する ■plagued with ～に苦しめられる

IMGアカデミーでの錦織のチームは、「プロジェクト45」と呼ばれていた。これは、それまで日本男子テニス界で最高位だった松岡修造の世界ランキング46位を上回るという目標を込めたプロジェクト名だった。錦織本人やIMGアカデミーのコーチ陣のみならず、盛田ファンドや日本テニス界が、松岡引退以来、ずっと目指してきた目標だ。

　その45位は、もう目の前だった。ボロテリーは錦織について、運動能力やフットワークの良さ、ラケットのヘッドスピードの速さ、球筋を予測する目、コートのセンスが優れているところ、度胸の良さを褒めたうえで、「彼にとって今もっとも大事なことは、ケガをしないこと」と断言した。健康さえ保てれば、ランキング45位を目指す錦織のチーム「プロジェクト45」は、すぐに「プロジェクト10」に改名されることになるだろう。誰もがそう思ったに違いない。しかしこのあと、錦織にとってケガに泣かされる、長く厳しいシーズンが待っていた。

The Beginning of Anguish

Kei achieved his personal-best no. 56 in the ATP rankings on February 2, 2009. In March, it was announced that he had received the 2008 ATP Newcomer of the Year award for his outstanding achievements during the previous year. This award is voted for by players on the ATP Tour.

Upon receiving the award, Kei said, "Every day I work incredibly hard to become one of the top players in the world and to get this recognition from fellow players means a lot to me."

The year 2009 seemed to be going great.

But in January, when he played at the Australian Open (where he was defeated in the first game), he felt a pain in his right elbow. He kept playing while nursing his elbow, but after the ATP World Tour Masters 1000 in Indian Wells in California, he ended up withdrawing from tournaments for the rest of 2009.

■outstanding 形傑出した　■previous 形前の　■vote 動投票する　■upon doing 〜するにあたって　■recognition 名真価を認めること　■fellow 名仲間　■mean a lot to 〜にとって意義深い　■nurse 動（怪我などを）かばう　■end up doing 結局〜することになる　■withdraw 動撤退する

苦悩の始まり

　錦織は、2009年2月2日付けで発表された世界ランキングで、自己最高の56位をマーク。翌3月には、前年1年間の活躍が認められ、2008年度のATPワールド・ツアー最優秀新人賞を受賞したことが発表された。この賞はATPツアーに参戦している選手からの投票によって決定される。

　アジア人初となった最優秀新人賞の受賞を受けて錦織は、「世界のトップ選手のひとりになるために、僕は毎日、ものすごい努力をしています。テニス仲間からこのような形で認めていただけることは、とても意義深いです」と談話を発表した。
　2009年はまさに順風満帆に思えた。
　しかし実は1月、全豪オープンに出場した際（1回戦で敗退）、右肘に痛みを覚えていた。肘をかばいつつプレーを続けたが、3月にカリフォルニア州インディアンウェルズで行われたATPワールドツアー・マスターズ1000を最後に、錦織は2009年、戦線から離れることとなった。

After the tournament in Indian Wells, Kei went to see a doctor, who found an inflammation. So Kei spent eight weeks in rehab. After that, he resumed racket training. But the pain didn't go away completely.

Kei couldn't make up his mind about the French Open until the last minute as he wasn't confident about playing five sets with his elbow. In the end, he withdrew from the tournament.

He still wanted to go to Wimbledon, so on May 20, he got MRI scans in New York as part of a complete checkup. It turned out that he had a stress fracture. As a result, he decided to take a rest for several months to concentrate on treatment.

■inflammation 图炎症　■rehab 图リハビリ　■make one's mind up 決心する
■until the last minute ギリギリまで　■checkup 图検査　■stress fracture 疲労骨折
■concentrate on 〜に専念する

インディアンウェルズでの大会のあとに医者に診てもらったところ、炎症が起きていると診断されたのだ。全仏オープンか全英オープンの出場を目指し、8週間のリハビリに専念した。その後、ラケットを使用した練習も開始した。ところが、痛みは完全に引かなかった。

　全仏オープンの出場をどうするか、ギリギリまで悩んだという錦織だったが、この肘でフルセットを戦える自信はなかった。結局、出場を断念することにした。

　しかし、全英オープンには出場したかったため、5月20日にニューヨークでMRIを使っての精密検査をしたところ、疲労骨折をしていたことが判明した。これを受けて、治療に専念するために2〜3カ月間は完全休養することになった。

Kei had suffered from minor injuries in his abdomen and lower back, but he didn't have any experience of such a big injury. Tennis players must keep getting in games to maintain their ranking. Taking a rest meant a drop in ranking. He had achieved his best of no. 56 in February 2009, but it fell to no. 116 on May 25 because he had been away from games since March. In a press interview held in Tokyo to announce time out due to injury, he repeated the word "frustrated," though he put on a smile. At the time of this press conference, he still had hopes that he could join the U.S. Open in August.

As it turned out, however, he couldn't make a comeback at the U.S. Open; instead, he had an operation in August. After that, he was out of action until February 2010.

At one point, Kei thought his career was over. He felt deep despair.

■abdomen 图腹部 ■lower back 腰 ■get in a game 出場する ■drop 图下降
■time out 中断 ■due to ～が原因で ■make a comeback 復帰する ■operation
图手術 ■out of action 活動していない

腹部や腰など、ケガに苦しんだことがないわけではなかったが、錦織はこれまで、これほど大きなケガをした経験はなかった。テニス選手は、ランキングを維持し続けるためには、試合に出場し続けなければならない。戦線から離れることはつまり、ランキングの下降を意味していた。2009年2月には自己最高の56位だったランキングは、3月以降試合に出ていないため、5月25日発表時には116位まで下がっていた。ケガによる休養を発表するために都内で行った記者会見では、笑顔を見せたものの「悔しい」という言葉を何度も口にした。この記者会見の時点では、8月の全米オープンにはまだ出場することができるかもしれない、という望みを持っていた。

　しかし結局のところ、全米オープンで復帰するどころか、8月には手術を受けることになってしまった。そしてこのあと、2010年2月まで約1年にわたり試合に戻ることはなかった。

　錦織は、このケガでもう自分のキャリアは終わりだと思ったときもあったという。それほど、精神的に追い詰められていたのだった。

Kei was undergoing rehab but getting frustrated because he had no prospects of playing in games, so Angus Mugford, a mental conditioning coach at IMG Academy, told him a story about Lance Armstrong.

Lance Armstrong is a former American cyclist. From 1993 to 1996, he won the World Championship and Tour DuPont as well as a stage of the Tour de France. But in 1996, he found out he had cancer. The doctors said his probability of survival was 50%. After that, Armstrong concentrated on treatment for a while, but he resumed training in 1998. From 1999 to 2005, he won the Tour de France seven times in a row.

This anecdote has a sequel. In 2012, Armstrong's drug taking was revealed and he was deprived of his seven Tour de France titles. However, when Mugford told Kei about Armstrong, the doping had not come out.

■undergo 動 (治療などを)受ける ■prospect 名 見通し ■find out 発見する
■probability of survival 生存率 ■in a row 連続して ■anecdote 名 逸話 ■sequel 名 続き ■deprive 動 剥奪する ■come out 判明する

IMGアカデミーのメンタル・コンディショニング・コーチであるアンガス・マグフォードは、リハビリテーションに励みつつも試合出場が見えずに焦る錦織に、ランス・アームストロングの話をして聞かせた。

　ランス・アームストロングとは、アメリカの元自転車ロードレース選手だ。1993年から1996年にかけて、世界選手権、ツアーデュポンでの優勝やツール・ド・フランスの区間優勝などで活躍。しかし1996年、がんに侵されていることが分かった。医者からは、生存率は50パーセントと宣告された。その後、アームストロングはしばらく治療に専念するが、1998年にトレーニングを再開。1999年から2005年にかけて、ツール・ド・フランスを7連覇した。

　実はこの逸話には続きがある。2012年になりアームストロングのドーピング違反が判明し、この7連覇ははく奪されているのだ。しかしマグフォードが錦織にこの話をしたときは、当然ながらまだドーピング違反は判明していなかった。

Mugford says he told this story to Kei because he wanted him to realize that "No one who has achieved success got there without experiencing setbacks." Kei did get over his injury and rejoiced because he was able to play tennis again. Also, his talent seemed to bloom because of that experience.

Moreover, van Lindonk says that he really learned about Kei's character while he was off due to injury for one year.

According to van Lindonk, Kei was at the Academy doing his rehabilitation and his gym work every day. He also paid his fees to his coach for the whole year, which most players would never do. Most athletes take five or six months off if they get injured. In his many years of experience, van Lindonk hasn't seen a lot of players who are as nice and good as Kei. According to van Lindonk, Kei is just a humble person, who really appreciates what he has. It would be hard to find someone who doesn't like him.

■setback 图挫折 ■get over 治癒する ■rejoice 動喜ぶ ■be off 離れる
■humble 形謙虚な ■hard to find ほとんどない

マグフォードがこの話を錦織に聞かせたのは、「成功した人たちとは、逆境を乗り越えた人たちだ」ということを、彼に知って欲しかったからだった。錦織はケガが癒えると、テニスをプレーできる喜びを噛みしめた。そして、その才能をさらに開花させたようだった。

　また、ケガで錦織が1年もの長きにわたって戦線から離れていたこの時期こそ、錦織の本質を知ることになった、とリンドンクは語っている。
　リンドンクによると、アカデミーに残った錦織は、毎日リハビリや筋トレを欠かさなかった。さらに、この1年間のブランクの間、なんとコーチにフィーを払い続けていた。こうしたことをする選手は、珍しいという。普通の選手なら、ケガをしたら半年間オフにしてしまうことが多いのだ。リンドンクはこれまでさまざまな選手を見てきたが、錦織ほど性格のいい選手はあまりいないという。自分が置かれた環境に心から感謝することができる、謙虚な男なのだ。錦織のことを嫌いだという人はほとんどいないだろう、とリンドンクは錦織の人間性を高く評価している。

覚えておきたい英語表現

> Kei lacked **confidence**. (p.60, 1行目)
> 錦織は自信がなかった。
>
> He said his **confidence** was shot. (p.68, 10行目)
> 自信はボロボロだったと話した。
>
> He wasn't **confident about** playing five sets. (p.78, 7行目)
> 彼はフルセットを戦える自信がなかった。

【用語】 lack confidence
　　　　 one's confidence is shot ｝自信がない
　　　　 be not confident about~

【解説】上述の3つの表現は、何か自信がないという気持ちを伝えたいときに役立つ表現です。2つ目の文のshotは「ボロボロになった」という意味の形容詞です。
　各種検定試験ではスピーキング、ライティング共にvocabulary（語彙）が評価基準の1つとして挙げられています。そのレベルに合った語彙が使えているか評価されるだけでなく、様々な語彙が使えているかも評価の基準になる（IELTSなど）場合もあります。つまり同じスピーチや、何か自分の意見を話す際に同じ単語を何回も使っていると、試験官はこの受験者は語彙力が乏しいと考える可能性があり、スピーキングやライティングの評価が下がる恐れがあります。普段から使いたい表現や単語の同義語も調べるようにしましょう。

【例文】 I am not confident about making a speech in front of the public.
　　　　聴衆の面前でスピーチをする自信がありません。

> To get this recognition from fellow players **means a lot to** me.
> (p.76, 9行目)
> テニス仲間からこのような形で認めていただけることは、とても意義深いです。

【用語】 mean a lot to~：~（人）にとって重要な意義がある、重要である

【解説】主語に人以外の名詞（無生物主語）がよく置かれるため、なかなかスピーキングの際に口から出にくい表現になっています。過去の出来事がどれだけ自分にとって重要だったか説明するときや、何か自分にとって重要な意味をもつことを示したいときに使える表現です。

【例文】 The experience I had when I was younger meant a lot to me.
若い頃に得た経験が私にとって重要なものになりました。

I don't want to break up with her as she means a lot to me.
彼女は大切な人なので、別れたくないです。

> No one who has achieved success got there without experiencing setbacks. (p.84, 2行目)
> 成功した人たちとは、逆境を乗り越えた人たちだ。

【解説】直訳すると「つまずきなしに成功した人はいない」という意味です。1つの文章にnoとwithoutがあり二重否定になっているので、強い肯定を示しています。個人的にこの物語の中でお気に入りのセンテンスです。うまくいかず、悩んでいる友人や家族、身近な人にこの言葉をかけてあげてください。

【例文】 Don't worry about your mistakes too much. No one who has achieved success got there without experiencing setbacks. You'll do great next time.
あまり自分の間違いを気にしないで。うまくいっている人たちは、逆境を乗り越えてきたんだよ。きっと次は大丈夫だ!!

Chapter 3
Restart

Meeting with Chang and Subsequent Advancement (2011–2014)

第3章
「再出発」

チャンとの出会いとその後の
快進撃（2011〜2014）

Kei made a comeback in 2010. Since he hadn't taken part in the game for one year, he started from no. 898, and later he dropped out of the rankings entirely. But he consistently played at ATP Challenger Tour events and improved his ranking step by step.

The year 2011 began by Kei getting his ranking to no. 98. This year saw two memorable events for Kei. First, after playing at the Shanghai Masters in October 2011, his ranking rose from no. 47 to no. 30, achieving the highest ranking record for a Japanese male player.

■take part in 〜に出場する ■consistently 副着実に ■step by step 少しずつ
■memorable 形記念すべき

錦織は2010年、戦線に復帰した。1年間にわたり試合に出場していなかったため、2010年は898位からスタートし、その後は圏外に落ちてしまった。しかしそれでも地道にチャレンジャー・ツアーに出場し、少しずつランキングを上げていった。

　2011年、ATPランキングを98位まで戻すことで年が明けた。この年、錦織にとって記念すべき出来事が2つ起こる。まずは2011年10月、上海マスターズが終わると、錦織はランキングをそれまでの47位から30位へと浮上させ、日本人男子としての最高位を更新するという快挙を達成した。

After Kei turned professional, his immediate goal was to attain a Top 100 ranking. But he had always aimed to place above no. 46, alien territory for Japanese male players. Four years after he turned professional, he managed to achieve this goal, though it wasn't the end of the story.

The instant Kei broke the record, "Project 45" turned into his next goal, "Project 10."

And in this same year, he had another momentous life event: meeting with Michael Chang, who would later become his coach.

Born in the U.S.A. on February 22, 1972, Michael Chang is a Taiwanese American and a former professional tennis player. When he was 17 years and 3 months old, he won the French Open. This record for the youngest champion of a Grand Slam hasn't been broken. He retired in 2003 and was inducted into the International Tennis Hall of Fame in 2008.

■alien territory 未知の領域　■managed to 何とか～する　■turn into ～に変わる
■momentous 形 重大な　■Hall of Fame 殿堂

錦織自身は、プロになって以来、まずは世界ランキング100位に入ることを目標としてきた。しかし錦織の頭には常に、日本男子にとって未達の域である世界ランキング45位以上になることがあったという。プロに転向して4年。その目標が、やっと達成できたのだった。しかし当然ながら、目標に到達したからといってここで終わるわけではなかった。

　錦織が日本人男子として最高ランキングの記録を更新したその瞬間に、「プロジェクト45」は、次の目標である「プロジェクト10」へと変わったのだった。

　そしてこの年、もう1つ大きな出来事があった。のちに錦織のコーチとなる、マイケル・チャンとの出会いだ。

　マイケル・チャンは、1972年2月22日にアメリカで生まれた、台湾系アメリカ人の元プロテニス選手だ。1989年、若干17歳3カ月にして全仏オープンで優勝した。グランドスラム優勝時のこの最年少記録は現在も破られていない。2003年に現役を引退し、2008年に国際テニス殿堂入りを果たしている。

In November 2011, Kei met Chang at the Dream Tennis exhibition match in Ariake Colosseum held in Koto Ward, Tokyo to raise funds for the Great Eastern Japan Earthquake.

Kei played against Chang in singles and doubles in "Dream Matches."

When they had time to chat during this event, Chang offered some advice to Kei. Chang pointed out that Kei had lacked in awareness and belief that he was one of the top players.

Chang said, "You're like a little boy looking up and there's Roger's poster on his wall."

Kei said to Chang that Federer was his idol and he looked up to him. He also told Chang how much he liked Federer.

Chang replied, "You know the way you're talking about Roger, I think that's all great and fine, but you know you are still competing against him, right?"

■exhibition match 模範試合《公式記録にならない試合》 ■ward 名区 ■raise funds for ～のために募金を集める ■chat 名雑談 ■awareness 名自覚 ■idol 名アイドル、崇拝の対象 ■right 間そうだよね

錦織とチャンは2011年11月、東京都江東区にある有明コロシアムで行われた、東日本大震災復興チャリティ・ドリーム・テニスARIAKEで出会った。

　ここで錦織は「ドリームマッチ」として、シングルスやダブルスでチャンと対戦した。
　このイベントで2人が世間話をしていた際に、チャンが錦織にアドバイスをしたことがあった。当時の錦織は、自分がトップ選手の一員であるという自覚や信念に欠けていた、とチャンは指摘する。
　「まるで少年が、壁に貼ったロジャー（フェデラー）のポスターを見上げているかのようでした」
　ロジャー・フェデラーは自分のアイドルであり尊敬している、と錦織は言い、いかにフェデラーを好きかという思いをチャンに語ったという。
　チャンはそれを聞いて、「ロジャーについて話してくれるのはいいんだけど、君はそれでもロジャーと対戦するわけだよね？」と錦織に返した。

Kei said, "Well, what do you mean?"

Then Chang said that he couldn't beat anybody if he had that kind of admiration for him. "You can't expect to go out and have this kind of admiration for somebody you are still competing against because if you do, you will never beat him."

11 At a Standstill Just Below the Top 10

Kei had fought against Federer in the Swiss Indoors held in Basel, Switzerland in October 2011. Kei, whose world ranking was no. 31 at that time, reached the semifinal where he performed a remarkable feat and defeated Novak Djokavic (Serbia), who was no. 1 at that time, and got to the final.

But his "secret idol" Federer was waiting there for him. This was before Kei met Chang, who pointed out that his perspective was wrong.

■admiration 图称賛　■expect to 〜するつもりである　■go out 〜に心が引かれる
■standstill 图停止　■feat 图業績　■perspective 图態度

錦織は「どういう意味ですか」といぶかしがったため、チャンは、「対戦する相手にそんな憧れを抱いていたら、その相手には絶対勝てないよ」とたしなめたという。

世界トップ10直前に足踏み

　実は、チャンと出会う直前の10月、スイスのバーゼルで行われたスイス・インドアで、錦織はそのフェデラーと対戦していた。当時世界ランキング31位だった錦織は準決勝まで順調に勝ち進み、当時1位だったノバク・ジョコビッチ（セルビア）を下すという大金星をあげ、決勝戦にまで進んだ。

　しかしここで決勝の相手となったのが、「憧れのアイドル」フェデラーだった。チャンと出会う前のことであり、「あの一言」でたしなめられる前だ。

Kei later confessed in an interview that his respect for Federer was so strong that he didn't have a strong desire to win, admitting that his mindset was the problem. Nishikori thought he was going to play against his idol, not an opponent to be beaten. It was inevitable that Kei was defeated in straight sets and Federer won the tournament in his home country, Switzerland.

Though Kei didn't win the Basel tournament, he kept producing good results now that he had recovered from his injury.

He continued to play steadily in 2012, and in October he won the Rakuten Japan Open. He became the first Japanese-born male player to have two victories on the ATP Tour. But his ranking got stuck around the mid to high teens.

In 2013, he won the U.S. National Indoor Tennis Championships (now named the Memphis Open) in Memphis, which brought him his third victory on the Tour. At the Mutua Madrid Open in Spain in May, he had a rematch against Federer and beat him.

■confess 動打ち明ける　■mindset 图考え方、物の見方　■inevitable 形当然の
■now that 今や〜だから　■get stuck 立ち往生する　■rematch 图再試合

このときはあまりにもフェデラーへの尊敬の思いが強すぎ、勝ちに行くという心持ちではなかったことを、錦織はのちにインタビューで告白している。これが当時の自分の問題だった、と。打ち負かすべき対戦相手というよりも、自分のアイドルとの試合だ、という思いが強すぎたのだ。当然ながら、錦織はストレート負けし、フェデラーが地元スイスで優勝を飾った。

　バーゼルでの優勝こそ逃したものの、ケガから復帰した錦織は、その後も順調に戦績を上げていった。

　2012年も堅調に試合をこなしていき、10月には楽天オープンで優勝。日本人男子初となるツアー2勝目を上げた。しかしランキングは10位台の中〜後半を行ったり来たりするにとどまった。

　2013年には、メンフィスで行われた全米国際インドアテニス選手権（現メンフィス・オープン）で優勝し、ツアー3勝目を上げた。5月にスペインで行われたムチュア・マドリード・オープンでは、あのフェデラーと再び対戦し、このときは勝利した。チャンの一言で錦織のマインドに変化があった可能性もあ

Chang's advice might have changed his mindset. In the rankings announced on June 17, he rose to his career-high, no. 11. It seemed that he would keep improving, but he had a hard time doing so and his ranking remained at no. 10-something.

In the latter half of 2013, Kei felt he should make a change. It occurred to him that he would need a new coach to get into the Top 10.

Kei had met Chang again at the French Open in May. At that time, Chang told Kei to contact him if there was anything he could do. But he didn't mean that he would work with Kei as a coach. Coming from an Asian heritage, he hoped to help increase the number of Asian tennis players. He wasn't looking for a coaching position.

But Kei's agent asked Chang to be his coach. Chang was inclined to help Kei, who shares a lot of similarities with him. In a later interview, he admitted that he didn't need to be a coach for financial reasons, saying, "You just do it because you want to do it."

■it seems that ～のように思える　■contact 動 ～に連絡する　■heritage 名 (生まれながらにして持つ) 地位、立場　■be inclined to ～したいと思う　■financial 形 金銭的な　■you 名 (誰か漠然とした) 人《日本語に訳されないことが多い》

るだろう。そして6月17日発表のランキングでは、自己最高位となる11位にまで浮上。このまま順調に順位を上げていくかのように思えた。しかしこのあと、なかなかランキングを上げることが出来ず、10位台をウロウロしていた。

　2013年の後半になると、錦織は何かを変えなければいけない、という思いにかられた。世界ランキング10位に入るために、新しいコーチが必要だという考えが頭に浮かび始めていた。
　錦織は5月に、全仏オープンでチャンと再会していた。そしてチャンはこのとき、「何か手助けできることがあったら声をかけてくれ」と錦織側に伝えていたのだった。このときのチャンの言葉の裏には、コーチとして、という意味はなかったという。「同じアジアにルーツを持つ選手として、もっとテニス界で活躍するアジア人選手を増やす力になりたい」という思いがあった。しかし、特にコーチの仕事を探していたわけではなかったのだ。
　しかし錦織のマネージャーは、チャンにコーチ業の打診を開始した。チャンにとって、自分と似た部分を多く持つ錦織を手助けしたいという思いは、大きかった。のちのインタビューで、とくに金銭的にはコーチ業をする必要性がまったくなかったことを認め、「やりたいからやるだけです」と語っている。

Chang had several reasons for wanting to help Kei. For one thing, as mentioned above, they were both of Asian descent, and Chang wanted to help Asian players find great success. Another key reason was that Kei was physically similar to Chang; Chang thought he could teach him some of the things that he had learnt on court.

Chang is 175 cm and Kei is 178 cm tall. They are also of small build for tennis players, as the taller the better. And they make up for their height handicap by their speed on court. Chang says that it would have been difficult to teach Kei as a coach if Kei were more than 2 meters. Kei could make use of what Chang had learnt on court because they are similar in body height and playing style.

Chang also experienced a similar situation when he was stuck around no. 15 in the rankings. It was around '89, '90 and '91, when he won the French Open. Then, his brother Carl started to coach him. This led his ranking to improve again, and in 1992, he managed to enter the Top 10. In 1996, he rose to his personal-best, no. 2.

■descent 图遺伝的特徴 ■find success 成功を手にする ■as the taller the better 背が高いほうがよい ■make up for (不足などの) 埋め合わせをする ■height 图身長 ■make use of ~を利用する ■stuck 形停滞した

チャンには、錦織を助けたいと思った理由がいくつかあった。ひとつは前述の通り、2人は同じアジアをルーツとしており、アジア人選手が活躍する力になりたいと思ったこと。また、体格が自分と似ているため、自分の経験を活かしたアドバイスができるのではないかと考えたのも、大きな理由だった。

　チャンは175センチメートル、錦織は178センチメートル。背が高い方が有利となるテニス選手としては、2人とも小柄な体格だ。そして、スピードでそれをカバーするスタイルのテニスを武器としている。もし錦織が2メートルを超えるような選手だったら、自分がコーチとして教えることには無理があっただろう、とチャンは語っている。チャンがコート上で実際に学んできたことを活かすことができるのは、背格好やプレースタイルが似ている錦織だからこそ、なのだ。
　またチャン自身、ランキングが15位前後で停滞し、苦しんだ時期があった。全仏オープンで優勝したあと、1989年、1990年、1991年のころだ。しかしそんなとき、チャンの兄カールがコーチ役を買って出てくれた。これがきっかけとなり、停滞していたランキングが再び動き出し、1992年には10位以内に到達することができた。その後1996年に自己最高ランキングとなる2位に到達した。

But Chang had never coached an ATP-class player before. Also, he knew how difficult the life of a professional tennis player was — they had to travel around the world. The time spent with Amber and his two daughters was the most important thing for Chang.

So Chang set a condition: to bring his family with him wherever he went. He thought this might break the deal as he knew none of the other coaches had families traveling with them, or at least, none of them were always accompanied by their family. But Chang couldn't compromise in this regard.

Yet Kei agreed readily to this. Chang says Kei gets along well with his daughters and it has been great. He also says that Chang's oldest daughter seems to make Kei smile more than any of the team members.

So, in December 2013, it was decided that Michael Chang would formally join "Team Nishikori." According to the announcement, Chang would work as a coach on a part-time basis in 2014, that is, for 17–20 weeks during the year. Kei kept Dante Bottini as his full-time coach, whom he had worked with for

■set a condition 条件を提示する ■deal 图取引 ■compromise 動譲歩する ■in this regard この点については ■readily 副すぐに ■get along with ～と仲良くする ■make someone smile （人を）笑顔にする ■on a part-time basis 時給制で

しかしチャンはこれまで、ATPクラスの選手へのコーチ経験は皆無だった。それに、世界中を回らなければならないプロテニス選手の生活がいかに大変かは、チャン自身が一番よくわかっていた。チャンにとって、元テニス選手である妻のアンバーと2人の娘たちと一緒にいる時間が、一番大切だった。

　そこでチャンは、錦織側に1つの条件を出した。「家族を帯同できること」。この条件で交渉が流れてしまう可能性も考えた。なぜなら、家族を帯同しているコーチなど、チャンは見たことがなかったからだ。少なくとも、常に家族を一緒に連れているコーチなどいない。しかし家族と一緒にいることは、チャンにとって絶対に譲れないポイントだった。

　しかし錦織は、二つ返事でこれを快諾した。「圭はうちの娘たちと仲良くしてくれているし、とてもうまくいっています」とチャンは話す。チャンの長女が、チームの誰よりも錦織を笑顔にしてくれるようだとも言っている。

　こうして2013年12月、マイケル・チャンが正式に「チーム錦織」に加わることが決まった。当時の発表によると、2014年は17〜20週というパートタイムのコーチ職だ。これまで4年間にわたり錦織をコーチしてきたダンテ・ボッティーニはフルタイムコーチとしてとどまり、3人で力を合わせてランキング10位以内を目指すこととなった。チャンは技術面のみならず、

about four years. The three-man partnership aimed at Kei breaking into the Top 10 in the ATP rankings. Chang was supposed to play an important role on the mental side of the game. Bottini said at the time that Chang "brings all the experience that he had as a player. We complement each other very well."

Tapping His Full Potential

After Chang became a coach, Kei took to something like a duck to water.

In February 2014, he won the U.S. National Indoor Tennis Championships (Memphis Open) again, winning his fourth Tour title. In March, he played against Federer again. As in the previous year, he won the match. In April, he won the Barcelona Open, marking the fifth Tour title of his career (and the second title that year).

■supposed to ～することになっている ■complement 動 補完する ■tap 動（能力などを）活用する ■like a duck to water カモが水に入るように極めてすんなりと

メンタル面でもサポートしていく予定だ。ボッティーニは、チャンについて「選手として培ったあらゆる経験を提供してくれます。私たちはお互いに補完しあういい関係です」と語った。

本領発揮

　チャンをコーチに迎えてからの錦織は、まるで水を得た魚のように本領を発揮し始めた。
　2月、前年に続き全米国際インドアテニス選手権（現メンフィス・オープン）を連覇し、ツアー4勝目を上げた。3月のソニー・オープンで、再びフェデラーと対戦し、2013年に続いて今回も勝利した。4月にスペインで行われたバルセロナ・オープンでは、ツアー通算5勝目、この年2度目となる優勝を飾った。

In May, Kei played in the Madrid Open. He defeated Raonic and Ferrer, and got to the final. His opponent was "King of Clay," Rafael Nadal. Kei took the first set, but due to a back injury he had to withdraw and took second place. But Kei later said this game was "the best in his career," and although he withdrew, he felt as if he were a winner. Nadal's coach, Toni Nadal, also admitted, "Nishikori played much better. It was not we, but he, that should have won."

And in the rankings announced on May 12, he broke into the Top 10 at no. 9. This feat was just five months after Kei had formally appointed Chang as a coach.

According to Chang, Kei clearly said at the outset, "One of my goals this year is to break into the Top 10."

■back 名背中 ■withdraw 動棄権する ■although 接〜ではあるものの ■as if まるで〜であるかのように ■not A, but B AではなくB ■appoint someone as (人を)〜に任命する ■at the outset 最初に

5月、マドリード・オープンに出場した錦織は、ラオニッチやフェレールを倒し、決勝戦まで駒を進めた。決勝の相手は「クレーの王者」、ナダルだ。1セット先行していたものの、背中の故障で泣く泣く棄権し、準優勝となった。しかし錦織はのちに、この試合を「これまでで一番のでき」とし、棄権はしたものの「まるで勝者の気分だった」と語っている。一方ナダルのコーチであるトニ・ナダルも、「錦織の方がずっといいプレーをしていた。勝つべきだったのは私たちじゃない。彼だった」と胸の内を明かしている。

　そして同じく5月、12日発表のランキングで、とうとう念願の10位以内となる9位に浮上した。チャンを正式にコーチとして迎えてわずか5カ月後の快挙だった。

　チャンによると、錦織は当初から「今年の目標はトップ10に入ること」と非常に明確にチャンに伝えていた。

Chang says that he doesn't think Kei expected it to happen that quickly, but also points out that he is quiet and reserved, does not go out partying or drinking, and is making tremendous effort toward what he wants to accomplish. He is not just talented, and it is a very good thing from a coach's standpoint. Kei's ability to accomplish what he wants clearly comes from this attitude.

Kei calls Chang a "tough" coach, but also says that he plays an important role on the mental side of the game. This aspect might be reflected in the fact that Kei, who had been just like a boy admiring Federer, won two consecutive victories over him after Chang pointed out it was the wrong way of thinking.

Now, he was set to appear in the 2014 U.S. Open, which all the tennis fans in Japan cannot easily forget.

■happen 動(予期せぬことが)起こる　■reserved 形 控えめな　■go out doing ～しに出歩く　■not just 単に～だけでなく　■good thing 望ましいこと　■consecutive 形 連続の　■be set to ～することになっている

「ここまで早く達成できるとは、本人も思っていなかったでしょうね」とチャンは話す。しかしチャンは、錦織がとても大人しく控えめで、騒いだり飲み歩いたりするような性格ではなく、目標に向かってものすごい努力をする選手であると指摘。才能があるだけではないのだ。それはコーチとして非常にありがたいことだとチャンは話す。そうした姿勢こそが、自らが定めた目標を着実に達成できる、錦織の強さなのだろう。

　錦織自身は、チャンについて「厳しいコーチ」と評価する。しかし技術面のみならず、ゲームにおけるメンタル面でも重要な役割を果たしてくれているという。それはチャンと出会った当初、フェデラーに憧れていた少年のようだった錦織が、チャンにたしなめられて以来、2戦連続でそのフェデラーに勝利していることからも伺える。
　そしてこの後、日本全国のテニス・ファンにとって忘れられない、2014年全米オープンを迎えることになる。

覚えておきたい英語表現

> Chang says Kei **gets along** well **with** his daughters.
> (p.104, 13行目)
> チャンは、圭がうちの娘たちと仲良くしてくれていると話す。

【用語】 get along with~：~と仲良くやっている、うまが合う

【解説】誰かと仲が良いと言いたいときに、get along with~という表現があります。特に家族や友人のことについて説明する文脈で使う機会も多いので、使えると便利でしょう。英検やIELTSなどのスピーキングのパートでも、身近な人について聞かれることがあります。

【例文】 How is your new company, Becky? Do you get along with your colleagues?
新しい職場はどうだい、ベッキー？　会社の同僚とはうまくやっているかい？

I used to get along well with my dad, but I don't often talk to him.
以前はお父さんと非常に仲が良かったけど、今はそんなに頻繁には話しません。

> Chang **was supposed to play an important role** on the mental side of the game. (p.106, 3行目)
> チャンは、精神面で重要な役割を担っていくことになっていた。

【用語】 be supposed to~：（約束や期待などによって）~することになっている
play an important role：重要な役割を果たす

【解説】be supposed to~を使うことで、ここではマイケル・チャンが、錦織のメンタル面の強化に寄与すると期待・予期されているというニュアンスになります。またplay an important roleで「重要な役割を果たす」という意味になり、何か重要であると言いたいときに使える便利な表現です。特にスピーキング

やライティングテストで使えるよう、暗唱しましょう。

【例文】 It is said that teacher education plays a crucial role in fostering better subject teaching.
教師教育は、より良い教科指導を促進するのに重要な役割を担っていると言われている。

The scientist played an important role in introducing clean energy in Japan.
その科学者は、日本でクリーンエネルギーを導入するのに重要な役割を担った。

Chapter 4
A Feat

Setting the Record as an Asian Male Player (2014)

第4章
「快挙」

アジア人男子初の記録
（2014）

On August 25, 2014, just before the U.S. Open which was to be held in New York, Kei wasn't in good condition physically. On August 23, just prior to the tournament, the local media reported that he was still suffering from an injury.

He hadn't played at the Rogers Cup in Canada and the Cincinnati Masters (the Western & Southern Open) in Cincinnati, which were held just before the U.S. Open, because he had had an operation to remove a cyst on his right foot. He even debated withdrawing.

Kei says he wasn't sure if his decision to play at the U.S. Open was right or not, and he was honest with the local media, telling them, "I'll take my chances on it." Also, he confesses that he felt he might not have been able to win his first round match because he was anxious about his physical condition.

■just prior to 〜の直前に　■cyst 图囊胞《中に液体がたまった袋状のしこり》
■debate 動討議する　■not sure if 〜かどうかよく分からない　■take one's chance on 〜を一か八かでやってみる　■be honest with 〜に正直に打ち明ける　■be anxious about 〜のことが不安で

2014年8月25日にアメリカのニューヨークで始まる全米オープンを前に、錦織の体調は思わしくなかった。直前の23日、現地メディアは「開幕直前、いまだケガに苦しむ錦織」と報じていた。

　全米オープン直前の大会となるカナダのロジャーズ・カップと、アメリカのシンシナティで行われるシンシナティ・マスターズ（ウエスタン・アンド・サザン・オープン）を欠場し、右足親指の嚢胞(のうほう)を摘出する手術を受けたのだ。全米オープンの出場も危ぶまれていた。

　錦織は、全米オープンに出場するという自らの決断が、はたして正しいものだったかどうか分からないとし、「一か八か出てみることにした」と正直な思いを現地メディアに話していた。さらに、体調面で不安が残るため、1回戦でさえも突破できるか分からない、と胸の内を語った。

Kei's coach Michael Chang urged Kei, who had cold feet, to play, saying, "Get past the first round, the second round, anything can happen."

But once the U.S. Open began, Kei made steady advances. He won in straight sets without losing a single set from the first round against Wayne Odesnik (the U.S.A.) to the second round against Pablo Andújar (Spain) to the third round against Leonardo Mayer (Argentina) (Andújar withdrew in the third set). It was as if the anxiety that he had shown just before the tournament was false.

In his fourth-round match, Kei played a great game that carved his name in the minds of tennis fans around the world. He went into a tough battle against Milos Raonic (Canada), who was ranked no. 6, somewhat higher than him. He needed five sets, which lasted four hours and 19 minutes, to beat Raonic. This was the longest match in the 2014 U.S. Open. The match ended at 2:26 a.m., equaling the record of the matches that had ended the latest in the long history of the U.S. Open that dates back to 1881. So far, Mats Wilander (Sweden) vs Mikael Pernfors

■have cold feet 躊躇する ■get past （難関などを）突破する ■make advance 前進する ■win in straight set 完全勝利する ■false 図 うそ ■carve one's name in ～に（人）の名前を刻み込む ■equal 動 ～に等しくなる ■date back to （起源などが）～までさかのぼる

迷う錦織に出場するよう勧めたのは、コーチのマイケル・チャンだった。「とにかく最初の2試合を勝ち進め。それができたら、何でも起こりうる」と錦織を励ました。

　しかし実際に全米オープンが始まってみると、錦織は快進撃を見せた。1回戦目のウェイン・オデスニック（アメリカ）、2回戦目のパブロ・アンドゥハル（スペイン）、そして3回戦目のレオナルド・メイヤー（アルゼンチン）まで、1セットも落とさずストレートで勝ち進んだ（2回戦目のアンドゥハルは3セット目で棄権）。まるで直前の不安な発言がうそのようだった。

　さらに4回戦目に進んだ錦織は、世界のテニス・ファンにその名を大きく印象づけるゲームをプレーした。当時ランキング6位と格上だったミロシュ・ラオニッチ（カナダ）との試合で、死闘を繰り広げたのだ。フルセットにもつれこんだ試合は、決着するまで実に4時間19分を要した。これは、2014年の全米オープンで最長の試合となった。また、試合終了のコールがコートに響いたのは、午前2時26分だった。これは1881年に始まった全米オープンの長い歴史のなかで、もっとも遅い時間に終わった試合のタイ記録だった。これまで、1993年のマッツ・ビランデル（スウェーデン）対ミカエル・ペルンフォルス（スウェーデン）と、2012年のフィリップ・コールシュライバー（ド

(Sweden) in 1993 and Philipp Eberhard Hermann Kohlschreiber (Germany) vs John Isner (U.S.A.) in 2012 are the only other two matches to have finished at 2:26 a.m. Thus Kei vs Raonic became only the third match to end at this time.

Interestingly enough, Chang, who is Kei's coach, is a record holder of the longest match in the history of the U.S. Open. In 1992, he played against Stefan Edberg in the semifinal for as long as five hours 26 minutes. In this match, Edberg beat Chang. Edberg now coaches Federer. This means that Chang and Edberg continued fighting as coaches through Kei and Federer after they retired as players.

Counting Kei's win, there have been five matches in U.S. Open history that ended after 2:00 a.m. All of the other four players who won a U.S. Open match that ended after 2 a.m. lost in the very next round of the tournament. This is understandable as the late night messes up the players' schedules completely. But for Kei it was different.

■thus 副 このように　■interestingly enough 大変興味深いことに　■record holder 記録保持者　■count 動 〜を数に入れる　■understandable 形 無理もない　■mess up （事態などを）めちゃくちゃにする

イツ）対ジョン・イスナー（アメリカ）の2試合が、午前2時26分に終了した。錦織のラオニッチとの試合はこれに並ぶもので、この時間に終了した3つ目の試合となった。

　興味深いことに、錦織のコーチであるチャンは、全米オープンの歴史における最長試合時間の記録保持者だ。1992年に準決勝でステファン・エドバーグと対戦し、5時間26分という長丁場を戦った。この試合ではエドベリが勝利した。このエドベリは現在、フェデラーのコーチとなっている。チャンとエドベリはつまり、現役を退いてもなお、今度はコーチとして、錦織とフェデラーを通じて対戦を続けていることになる。

　全米オープンの歴史のなかで、試合終了が午前2時を過ぎたゲームは、これまで5試合ある。この年の錦織とラオニッチとの試合をのぞくと、4試合ということだ。そこで勝利を手にした4人の選手は全員、勝ち進んだ次の試合で敗退している。深夜までかかってやっと勝ち取った試合だ。スケジュールも狂ってしまうし、体力の限界まで戦ったであろうから、無理もない。しかし、錦織は違った。

Kei ended the match at 2:26 a.m., on Tuesday September 2, and after talking to the media, he went back to his hotel in Manhattan after 4 a.m. He didn't get to bed until close to 6 a.m. that morning. But his next match was a day match on the Wednesday. His opponent was Stan Wawrinka, who was ranked no. 4, even higher than Raonic. He had won the Australian Open earlier that year, and it was the first Grand Slam title for him. Kei was seemingly at a disadvantage. Moreover, he wasn't sure about his physical condition as he had said at the beginning of the U.S. Open that he might not be able to move quickly as he had recently had an operation.

Chang was concerned about another thing on top of the injury. He thought Kei might still be focusing on the Raonic match and ecstatic about the victory. His mind might not have moved on to the next match against Wawrinka. As already mentioned, no players with a big win had been successful in the next round. As Chang points out, this might be due to physical issues, but also due to their mind being occupied with the victory of the previous match.

■close to ほぼ〜 ■day match 日中の試合 ■seemingly 副 見たところ ■on top of 〜の他に ■focus on 〜に心を向ける ■ecstatic 形 酔いしれた ■move on to 〜に移行する ■be occupied with 〜でいっぱいである

2日火曜日、午前2時26分に試合を終えた錦織は、その後メディア対応などに追われ、マンハッタンの宿泊先に戻ることができたのは、午前4時をまわっていた。やっと就寝できたのは、まもなく午前6時になろうという時間だったという。錦織の次の試合は、水曜日のデイゲーム。対戦相手は、世界ランキングではラオニッチのさらに上をいく4位（当時）のスタン・ワウリンカ（スイス）だ。この年の1月全豪オープンを制して、自身初のグランドスラム・タイトルを手にしたばかりの選手だ。錦織は、条件的には不利だと思われた。しかも手術からまだ日が浅い全米オープン開幕当初は、「素早い動きはできないかもしれない」と口にしていたほど、体調に不安があった。

　チャンには、ケガの他にも気がかりなことがあった。ラオニッチとの死闘があまりにも印象的すぎて、錦織の心はまだその勝利に酔いしれているかもしれない。ワウリンカとの試合に向けて、気持ちが切り替わっていないかもしれないのだ。前述の通り、長時間の試合を競り勝った選手が次の試合で勝てたケースはなかった。体力的なこともあるだろうが、チャンが指摘するように、前の試合の勝利で頭がいっぱいになってしまうという精神状態が原因であることもあるだろう。

So, to keep him focused, Chang told Kei, "You've got another match to play here," and "The tournament isn't done yet."

In the match against Wawrinka, Kei fought five sets for more than four hours again. Two big matches in three days. The match that day took four hours 15 minutes. But Kei stood there as the winner again. After the match he said with a broad smile, "I don't know how I won. But I'm very happy." Wawrinka was impressed by Kei's persistence.

14 Defeating the World No. 1 to Reach the Final of a Grand Slam for the First Time

On September 6, 2014, a Saturday, New York was humid and hot. Kei's opponent in the semifinal was the mighty monarch Novak Djokovic, who was ranked no. 1.

■done 形完了した ■broad smile 満面の笑顔 ■be impressed by 〜に感銘を受ける
■persistence 名粘り強さ ■humid 形むしむしする ■mighty 形強力な ■monarch
名王者

そこでチャンは、「まだこなすべき試合は残っている」、「まだ大会は終わっちゃいないぞ」と声をかけ、集中力をきらさないように気をつけたという。
　実際にワウリンカとの試合が始まってみると、錦織はこの日、再び4時間以上におよぶ5セット・ゲームを行うことになった。わずか3日間のうちに2回目だ。この日の試合は、4時間15分かかった。しかし錦織はまたもや、勝者としてコートに立っていた。試合後、「どうやって勝ったのか、自分でもよく分からない。でもすごく嬉しいです」と満面の笑みを浮かべた。ワウリンカは、錦織の粘り強さを賞賛した。

世界ナンバーワンを破り
初のグランドスラム決勝へ

　2014年9月6日土曜日、ニューヨークは蒸し暑かった。
　準決勝戦に進んだ錦織の対戦相手は、世界ランキング1位、無敵の王者ノバク・ジョコビッチだ。

In this year, Djokovic was the vice champion in the French Open and the champion in Wimbledon. In the U.S. Open, he had reached the final for four consecutive years from 2010 to 2013, and won the title in 2011.

In contrast, Kei hadn't recorded any significant achievements in Grand Slams. He hadn't particularly garnered much attention overseas until he was nicknamed the "Marathon Man" by the foreign media because of the tenacity he had shown in the previous two matches. Moreover, due to the operation he had undergone just before, he had only started to go into serious training several days before the U.S. Open. At first, his physical condition was such that he didn't even know if he would go to New York. Even those who were unfamiliar with tennis would have most probably expected a Djokovic victory.

However, the result reversed the expectations of many people. Kei won the match to reach the final of the U.S. Open, or a Grand Slam, as the first Japanese or Asian male player.

■vice champion 準優勝　■in contrast その一方　■significant 形 いちじるしい
■garner 動 (注目などを)集める　■tenacity 図 粘り強さ　■be unfamiliar with ～をよく知らない

ジョコビッチはこの年、全仏オープンは準優勝、全英オープンでは優勝を飾っていた。全米オープンでは、2010年から2013年まで4年連続で決勝戦に進んでおり、うち2011年には優勝していた。

　一方の錦織は、これまでグランドスラムで目立った戦績はない。さらに、この前の2試合で見せたその粘り強さから、海外メディアに「マラソンマン」というニックネームをつけられるまで、とりたてて海外で注目されることもあまりなかった選手だった。さらに、直前に受けた手術の影響から、この全米オープンが始まるわずか数日前にやっと本格的な練習を開始したくらいで、「（全米オープンの会場がある）ニューヨークに行くかどうかさえ、自分でも分からなかった」という状態からのスタートだった。テニスに詳しくなくても、多くの人はジョコビッチの勝利を予測しただろう。

　しかし実際は、多くの人たちの予想を裏切るものとなった。錦織が、日本人男子として、そしてアジア出身の男子として初めて、全米オープン、さらにはグランドスラムの決勝に進むことになったのだ。

Nishikori only lost in one set to Djokovic. The temperature during the match reached 32°C. Players on the court would have felt much hotter. After the match, Djokovic did an interview and candidly said that it was not easy to play in these conditions. But he also mentioned that Kei spent more hours on the court than him, so that the heat was no excuse.

On the other hand, Kei said he felt great because he had beaten the world no. 1 player. He was giving a sober analysis of the match he had just played, but when the interviewer said, "You are going to be the first Japanese male player to play in the final in the Majors. What do you think the response will be from Japan?" He smiled broadly and said with gusto, "I hope it's big news in Japan. I feel the support from Japan even from the TV, and even though it's 4 o'clock in the morning I hope a lot of people are watching." Sure enough, the whole world was filled with delight, and his victory made the headlines.

■candidly 副率直に ■be no excuse 言い訳にならない ■sober analysis 冷静な分析
■gusto 図心からの喜び ■sure enough 思ったとおりに ■make a headline 大ニュースになる

試合は、ジョコビッチ相手に1セットを落としただけだった。試合中の気温は32度に達していた。コート上はもっと暑く感じただろう。試合後、ジョコビッチはインタビューに答え、この環境で試合をするのは簡単じゃなかった、と正直な思いを語った。しかしこの全米オープンでの錦織の合計試合時間がジョコビッチを上回るものであったことに言及。言い訳にはならない、と自らを戒めた。

　一方で錦織は試合後のインタビューで、世界ナンバー1プレーヤーを破って素晴らしい気分だと話した。今終わったばかりの試合を冷静に振り返って分析していた錦織だが、インタビュアーが「メジャー大会の決勝戦に出場する初めての日本人男子となりますが、日本での反応はどうだと思いますか」という質問を投げかけると、顔をくしゃくしゃにほころばせ、嬉しそうに次のように語った。「大きなニュースになっていると嬉しいです。日本からものすごいサポートを感じます。日本は今、朝の4時だけど、たくさんの人が見ているといいな」。間違いなく、日本では国中が喜びに包まれ、大ニュースになっていた。

The U.S. Open Final Without the Big Four

The final took place on Monday, two days after the semifinal. The opponent was Marin Cilic (Croatia), who had won a straight victory against Roger Federer in the other semifinal.

Since Federer had won a Grand Slam for the first time in 2003 Wimbledon, almost all the Grand Slam titles had been taken by one of the "Big Four" for 12 years, that is, before the 2014 Wimbledon. The only Grand Slam titles the Big Four didn't win since 2004 were the 2004 French Open, the 2005 Australian Open and the 2009 U.S. Open. Furthermore, the only finals that took place without a member of the Big Four were the 2004 French Open and the 2005 Australian Open. The Big Four members are, of course, Novak Djokovic, Roger Federer, Andy Murray (U.K.) and Rafael Nadal (Spain), all of whom are rated at the highest level. These mighty four champions had ruined other players' dreams of winning a Grand Slam title.

■take place 行われる ■win a straight victory ストレート勝ちする ■rate 動 ～を格付けする ■ruin 動 ～を破壊する

ビッグフォー不在の全米オープン決勝

　決勝戦は、準決勝から1日おいた月曜日に行われた。相手は、準決勝でロジャー・フェデラーをストレートで破ったマリン・チリッチ（クロアチア）だ。

　2003年の全英オープンでフェデラーが初めてグランドスラムの頂点に立ったのを皮切りに、2014年全英オープンまでの12年間は、男子のグランドスラムはほぼすべて、「ビッグフォー」のいずれかが優勝をさらってきた。2004年以降のグランドスラムでビッグフォー以外の選手が勝ったのは、2004年の全仏オープンと2005年の全豪オープン、そして2009年の全米オープンだけだ。また、ビッグフォーがいない顔合わせとなる決勝戦は、実に2004年の全仏オープンと2005年の全豪オープンだけだった。ビッグフォーとは言わずと知れた、世界ランキング上位に名を連ねるノバク・ジョコビッチ、ロジャー・フェデラー、アンディ・マレー（イギリス）、ラファエル・ナダル（スペイン）の4人である。この不動の王者4人が分厚い壁となって、他の選手のグランドスラム優勝の夢を阻んできた。

But in 2014, the unbeatable Big Four began to crack. In the Australian Open, Wawrinka won the tournament. And at the final of the U.S. Open, the tenth seed Kei and the 14th seed Cilic appeared on court. The year 2014 appears to have ushered in a generational change. The younger players who tried to challenge the Big Four started to be called the "New Wave." Later in an interview, Djokovic mentioned some examples of this "New Wave" as Cilic, Wawrinka, Nishikori, Raonic, and Grigor Dimitrov.

Either player could have won the 2014 U.S. Open final. Kei caught a wave in this tournament and he had won five out of seven matches against Cilic previously. Moreover, he had had three consecutive victories over Cilic including two matches in 2014. But Kei had already spent 16 hours and 26 minutes on court since the U.S. Open started. On the other hand, Cilic had spent 14 hours and 49 minutes. Also, Nishikori had had two five-set matches in a row. A lot of Japanese tennis fans would have worried about his stamina.

■unbeatable 形 無敵の　■crack 動 ひびが入る　■appear to ～するように思われる
■usher 動 ～の先駆けとなる　■catch a wave 波に乗る　■including 前 ～を含めて

しかし2014年、ビッグフォーの無敵の強さに陰りが見えてきた。全豪オープンでは、ワウリンカが優勝を手にした。全米オープンの決勝も、第10シードの錦織と第14シードのチリッチの顔合わせとなったのだ。2014年は、新旧交代を予感させる年になったと言えるだろう。そして、こうしたビッグフォーの一角を崩そうと迫る若い選手たちは、「ニューウェーブ」と呼ばれはじめていた。のちにジョコビッチはとあるインタビューで、この「ニューウェーブ」の例として、チリッチ、ワウリンカ、錦織、ラオニッチ、グリゴール・ディミトロフ（ブルガリア）の名をあげた。

　この「ニューウェーブ」同士の対戦となる2014年の全米オープン決勝戦は、どちらが勝っても不思議はなかった。錦織はこのトーナメントで波に乗っていた。また、チリッチとはこれまで7回戦い、5回勝利していた。しかも2014年に戦った2試合を含め、3戦連勝中だ。ただ、全米オープンが始まってから、錦織はここまですでに16時間26分をコートで過ごしていた。対するチリッチは14時間49分。しかも錦織は2試合連続でフルセットのゲームをしており、体力的に大丈夫なのだろうか、という不安を日本のテニス・ファンの多くは抱いていただろう。

The final match turned out to be a one-sided match, and Cilic won a straight sets victory over Kei. Especially, 198-cm-tall Cilic, hit powerful serves at over 200 km an hour. Cilic got his first Grand Slam title.

Japanese fans watched the match in suspense on TV in their home or sports pubs early in the morning because of the time difference. Kei could not become the first Japanese to win a Grand Slam, but they expressed open admiration and felt pride in the feat of Kei, the first Japanese and Asian who had reached the championship round of the U.S. Open.

After the U.S. Open, Kei won the Malaysian Open and the Rakuten Japan Open, his 7th career title. His ranking rose to no. 6.

Playing at the World Tour Finals as the First Asian Male

In October 2014, Kei was able to play at the World Tour Finals as the first Asian male player.

■turn out to be 結局は〜という結果になる　■one-sided 形 一方的な　■in suspense 一喜一憂して　■time difference 時差　■open admiration 心からの称賛　■feel pride in 〜を誇りに思う　■championship round 決勝戦

実際に決勝戦が始まってみると、一方的な試合展開となり、チリッチがストレートで錦織を退けた。とくに198センチメートルという長身のチリッチが放つ、時速200キロメートルを超えるサーブの強さが目立った。チリッチは、自身初のグランドスラム・タイトルを手にした。

　日本のファンは、時差の関係で早朝となった試合を、自宅やスポーツパブのテレビで一喜一憂しながら観戦した。日本人初のグランドスラム優勝とはならなかったものの、日本人そしてアジア人の男子選手として初めての快挙に、日本のファンは錦織の健闘を心から称え、誇りに思った。

　錦織はこのあと、マレーシア・オープンと楽天オープンを連覇し、ツアー通算7勝目をあげた。ランキングは6位に浮上した。

アジア男子初、ワールド・ツアー・ファイナル出場

　2014年10月、錦織は、アジア人男子選手初となるATPワールド・ツアー・ファイナルに出場できることとなった。

The ATP World Tour Finals is literally an event that wraps up the year of ATP World Tours. Only eight players, including the Grand Slam champions of the year, and selected top-ranked players can play there.

Unlike a normal tournament, the eight players are divided into two groups of four, and play a round robin in their group. The top two in each group advance to the semifinals. The first-placed player in one group plays against the second-placed player in the other group, and the two winners play in the final.

The 2014 event was held at the O2 Arena in London, U.K. from November 9 through 16. The fourth seed Kei came off second best in Group B and advanced to the semifinal, where he would play against Djokovic, the top player in Group A. On the other hand, Wawrinka, the second in Group A would play against Federer, the top player in Group B. The winners would play in the final.

■literally 副文字通り　■wrap up 締めくくる　■be divided into 〜に分けられる
■round robin 総当たり戦　■first-placed 形1位の　■come off （順位などが）〜という結果になる

ATPワールド・ツアー・ファイナルとはその名の通り、ATPワールド・ツアーの1年間の最後を締めくくる大会だ。その年のグランドスラム優勝者やランキング上位者から選ばれた8選手のみが出場を許される。

　通常のトーナメント戦と異なり、まず8人を2グループに分け、ここで総当たり戦を行う。グループでの勝者2人の計4人がそれぞれ準決勝に進み、グループの1位が他グループの2位と試合をし、そこで勝った2人が決勝で優勝を争うことになる。

　2014年の大会は、11月9日から16日まで英国ロンドンのO2アリーナで開催された。第4シードで出場した錦織は、Bグループ2位となり準決勝に駒を進め、Aグループ1位のジョコビッチと対戦することになった。その一方で、Aグループ2位のワウリンカとBグループ1位のフェデラーが対戦。この勝者同士が、決勝で優勝をかけて対戦する。

Kei progressed to the semifinal in his first event, but lost to Djokovic by 1–2, like revenge for the U.S. Open. The final was played by old faces, Djokovic and Federer. But Federer withdrew due to a back injury, and Djokovic won by default. In the 45-year history of the ATP World Tour Finals (including former events under different names), it was the first time a player won without playing the final.

Partly because of his achievement in this ATP World Tour Finals, Kei ended the year of 2014 with a career-high world ranking of no. 5.

■progress to ～に達する　■old faces お馴染みの顔ぶれ　■win by default 図不戦勝になる　■partly because of ～が理由の一つで

錦織は、初出場で準決勝進出と大健闘したものの、まるで全米オープンの仇(かたき)を取られるかのように、ジョコビッチに2-1でねじ伏せられた。決勝は、ジョコビッチとフェデラーというお馴染みの顔合わせとなった。しかしフェデラーが背中を負傷していたため棄権し、ジョコビッチの不戦勝となった。ATPワールド・ツアー・ファイナルの45年間の歴史（名称が異なる旧大会を含む）で、決勝戦を行わずに勝者が決まったのは初めてのことだった。
　このATPワールド・ツアー・ファイナルでの活躍もあり、錦織は自己最高記録となる世界ランキング5位で2014年を締めくくった。

覚えておきたい英語表現

> The late night **messes up** the players' schedules completely.
> （p.120, 下から3行目）
> 深夜（までかかる試合）は選手のスケジュールを完全にめちゃくちゃにする。

【用語】　mess up：台無しにする、ちらかす

【解説】mess upを英英辞典でひくと、to make something dirty or badlyとなり、日本語にすると「汚くする、台無しにする」という訳になります。ここでは深夜にまで及ぶ長時間の試合が選手のスケジュール管理に多大な影響を与えていることが、mess upが使われることによって見事に表されていますね。またhave a mess / make a messも「ちらかす、ごちゃごちゃにする」という意味になります。

　余談ですが、ブルーノ・マーズの"Young Girls"の歌詞に、You make a mess of me.（あなたは私をおかしくする）という意味でmake a messが使われています。

【例文】　I messed up a lot of questions in the exam due to lack of sleep.
　　　　睡眠不足のため多くの問題を解くことができなかった。

　　　　I often have a mess in my room.
　　　　よく自分の部屋をちらかしてしまう。

> He hadn't particularly **garnered** much **attention** overseas.
> （p.126, 7行目）
> 彼はとりたてて海外で注目されることもあまりなかった選手だった。

【用語】　garner attention：注目を集める

【解説】ある人物や企業が注目を集めていると言いたいとき、どういった表現が

あるでしょうか？　このチャプターではgarner attentionを使って「注目を集める」と表しています。他には、getやreceive attentionで「注目を集める」と表現できます。同じような表現を調べるときのオススメのサイトは、Online Oxford Collocation Dictionary (http://www.freecollocation.com) です。無料でコロケーションを調べることができるだけでなく、簡単に同様の表現も調べることができます。

【例文】 The celebrity garnered significant attention from the media.
その有名人はメディアから大きな注目を集めた。

The company began to receive considerable attention on TV.
その会社はテレビで多くの注目を集め始めた。

These mighty four champions had **ruined** other players' **dreams** of winning a Grand Slam title. (p.130, 下から3行目)
この不動の王4人が分厚い壁となって、他の選手のグランドスラム優勝の夢を阻んできた。

【解説】ruinは「台無しにする、機会などをつぶす」という意味の動詞です。ここではBig 4と言われた4人のランキング上位者が、他のプレーヤーのグランドスラム優勝という悲願を台無しにする、つまり大きな壁となって立ちはだかるというニュアンスになります。ruin one's dreamは、自分の口からなかなか出てきにくい表現だと思うので、暗唱しましょう。

【例文】 The pressure from her parents ruined her dream of becoming a singer.
両親からの重圧が歌手になりたいという彼女の夢を阻んだ。

Chapter 5
The Future

Kei's Goals
(2015–)

第5章
「未来」

錦織の目指すところ
(2015〜)

Kei reached a milestone in his career in 2014. But a few people believe that he would have achieved this much earlier had he not been injured. He would often suffer injuries — he improved his ranking, only to decline again due to an injury and in May 2014, he had to withdraw with a title before his very eyes at the Madrid Open.

According to his coach Bottini, Kei has worked hard to build his strength, spending many hours in the gym, especially on weight-training.

Mental Toughness

Bollettieri further points out that Kei's biggest problems have sometimes been in his head. But this is where Chang has helped him. Bollettieri believes Chang has made him very competitive and willing to fight in every match. There used to be times when he

■milestone 名金字塔、人生の節目　■decline 動低下する　■before one's very eyes 目前に　■build strength 体を鍛える　■competitive 形競争心の強い　■willing to 〜 に前向きである

2014年は錦織のキャリアの中でも金字塔となる戦績を残した1年だった。しかし「もしケガがなければ、もっと早い段階でこのような活躍ができただろう」と分析する声も少なくない。錦織はこれまで、せっかく上げたランキングを下げてしまったり、2014年5月のマドリード・オープン決勝で優勝を目前に棄権を余儀なくされたりと、ケガに泣かされたことが多かった。

　コーチのボッティーニによると、錦織はここのところ、ケガをしない体づくりを目指し、ジムでウェイト・トレーニングを多く行い、筋力・体力をつける努力をしてきたという。

メンタルの強さ

　ボロテリーはさらに、これまで錦織の一番の弱さはケガではなく、精神面だったと指摘する。だが、まさにそこそこが、チャンがチーム錦織に加わって以来、効果を発揮している部分だった。ボロテリーから見ても、チャンのおかげで錦織はかなり競争心を見せるようになってきた。毎試合、勝ちへの意欲が

would throw in the towel. But two consecutive five-set matches should be proof that he has overcome his mental weakness.

Kei's coach Bottini sometimes feels bothered by laid-back Kei. Bottini once told an anecdote where Kei always falls behind in the airport. His staff always looks for him. He's so slow that it irritates Bottini sometimes. But if Kei wants to save the energy for the matches by going slow, that's fine with him, Bottini says.

Going his own way is, in a sense, his strength. But in some instances, it could become his worst enemy. Chang tries to encourage him to be a little more intense, a little more pumped up.

Also, Chang tries to make Kei understand how important it is to believe in his own potential. Of course, Kei has put in lots of hard work, but if he doesn't believe that he can do something, he will never be able to do it, regardless of how skilled he is. "That's how important the mental side of tennis is," Chang says.

■throw in the towel 諦める　■proof 图証し　■feel bothered わずらわしく思う　■laid-back 圈のんびりした　■fall behind 遅れをとる　■go one's own way マイペースで行く　■in a sense ある意味で　■pumped up 熱狂した　■regardless of 〜にかかわらず

伝わってくるようになった。それまでは、ムリだと思うと諦めてしまうところがあったのだという。しかし2014年全米オープンで、2試合連続でフルセットを戦ったあの粘りは、まさにこうした精神面での弱さを克服できた証しといえるだろう。

のんびりとした錦織の性格について、ボッティーニはときに苦労するという。こんなこぼれ話を明かしたことがある。移動の際に、錦織は空港でいつものんびりと一番後ろを歩いているのだ。あまりにも遅すぎて姿を見失うことさえあり、そんなときスタッフは錦織を探すはめになる。ボッティーニはそれでイライラさせられることがあるというのだ。しかしのんびりと行動することで試合へのエネルギーをセーブしているのなら、まったく構わない、とボッティーニは言う。

こうしたマイペースなところは、ある意味、錦織の強さでもある。しかし時と場合によっては、弱点になってしまう場合もあるようだ。チャンは、もう少しアグレッシブになるよう錦織に指導しているという。

さらに、自分の可能性を信じることがいかに大切であるかについて、チャンは錦織に理解してもらおうとしている。もちろん、錦織は常に多大な努力をしている。しかし何かについて、「自分はできるんだ」と信じきっていないと、たとえどれだけ技術を持っていようと、できるようにはならない。「テニスにおけるメンタル面というのは、それほど重要なのです」とチャンは話す。

Kei himself also says Chang is helping him greatly on the mental side. Chang tells him to stay focused during the match, to never get too frustrated. According to Kei, Chang always pumps him up. Chang always congratulates him but also says, "It's not done yet. Stay focused."

Kei says he can learn a lot from Chang. Sometimes he has differences with Chang, but he tries to discuss these and understand what he thinks. Kei says Chang is one of the reasons he came to believe in himself and feel certain that he could beat Top 10 players. Thanks to Chang, he is calmer on court and his concentration is much better now.

Also, Kei says he is now playing more aggressively thanks to Chang. He used to be waiting for the opponent's misplay. But now, he uses his forehand more and tries to move forward.

Kei has great confidence in Chang probably because Chang has also stood on court as a player, felt the same pressure, and seen the same world as him. Chang gives advice from the experiences he has had, so it is most credible.

■stay focused 集中力を保つ　■pump someone up (人を)奮い立たせる　■feel certain 確信する　■thanks to 〜のおかげで　■misplay 図(スポーツにおける)ミス、エラー　■move forward 前に進む　■credible 形信頼できる

錦織自身も、チャンのメンタル面でのサポートは非常に大きいと語ったことがある。試合に集中すること。試合中にフラストレーションをため込みすぎないこと。チャンからそう指導されている。錦織によると、チャンは常に錦織をうまく奮い立たせてくれる。そしていつも試合後には、おめでとうとは言ってくれるものの、「まだ終わってはいない。集中力を切らしてはダメだ」と言って気を抜かないよう声をかけてくれるのだ。

　錦織は、チャンから多くのことを学べる、と話す。考え方が異なるときもあるが、話をして、チャンの考え方を理解しようと努力するのだという。自分を信じることができるようになったこと、そして自分はトップ10の選手にも勝てるのだという自信を持てるようになったことも、チャンのおかげだと話す。また、以前よりも試合中に集中できるようになり、落ち着いていられるようになったという。

　錦織はまた、より攻撃的なテニスができるようになったのも、チャンの指導のおかげだとしている。これまでは、相手のミスをひたすら待ってしまうところがあった。しかし今は、もっと自分のフォアハンドを使い、もっと前に出るように努力するようになったという。

　こうしてチャンに絶大な信頼を寄せるのも、やはりチャン自身がかつて選手として、実際に同じコートに立ち、同じプレッシャーを感じ、同じ世界を見てきたからだろう。体験にもとづいたものほど、信ぴょう性の高いアドバイスはない。

Kei's former mentor Shuzo Matsuoka, Nick Bollettieri at IMG Academy and many others who have kept a close eye on Kei call him a "genius."

In men's tennis, the ball from a tall body is a strong weapon. But Kei is relatively short. But he has survived with excellent ball control, quick motion, and his trademark "Air K" and great forehand. But it is not enough to be a champion of the men's tennis world.

Chang works with Kei on both his technical and mental improvement, and stresses how emotional strength is required in a tennis player. To lift the trophy of a Grand Slam, it is not enough to have as good a technique as possible. Only when you have mental toughness can you reach the top of more than 2,000 tennis players in the ATP rankings.

After being defeated by Cilic in the 2014 U.S. Open, Kei said: "I can beat, you know, any player, that I believe. So (I will) have to stay really focused all the time and prepare well and just play good tennis on court."

■mentor 图良き指導者　■keep a close eye on ～を見守る　■relatively 副比較的に
■stress 動～を強調する　■you know ええと、あの《言葉につまったときなどの間投句》

錦織の恩師・松岡修造しかり、IMGアカデミーのニック・ボロテリーしかり、錦織を間近で見守ってきた人物で、錦織のことを「天才」と表現する人は多い。

　長身から繰り出す球が強力な武器となる男子テニス界において、比較的背の低い錦織。そこを、抜群のボールコントロールと機敏な動き、そして錦織の代名詞ともなっている「エア・ケイ」を含む得意のフォアハンドで戦い抜いてきた。しかし男子テニス界に君臨する王者になるには、それだけでは十分ではないのだ。

　技術面だけでなく、錦織のメンタル面の強化にも取り組んでいるチャンは、いかに精神的な強さがテニス選手には必要かを強調する。グランドスラムの優勝トロフィーを持ち上げるためには、誰にも負けない技術を持っているだけではだめなのだ。精神面でも崩れない強さを持ち合わせて初めて、グランドスラムという大舞台で、ATPランキングに名を連ねる2千人強のテニス選手の頂点に立つことができる。

　2014年の全米オープンで、チリッチに負けたあとの記者会見で、錦織はこんなことを口にした。

　「今の僕なら、どんな相手にも勝てる可能性があるんだということを示せたと思います。だから、トレーニングを重ねて練習をがんばれば、もっと（勝つための）チャンスが出てくると思います」

In the interview after he beat Raonic two matches earlier, he said in the Japanese language, "I think there is no player I cannot beat." Many of you may remember that it was much talked about.

Kei used to look shy and humble, but after the U.S. Open he came to believe in his abilities and openly express his self-confidence. He genuinely believes it when he says, "I am no longer a player who stares longingly at leading players from a distance. Now I am one of the top gun players."

Several months later, in the ATP World Tour Finals, the selfie photo by Tomáš Berdych with all his rivals was made public. Kei is smiling broadly in the front row as if to show his self-confidence. This is no longer the boy who looked up to the poster of his idol player, a naïve side about him pinpointed by Chang. As a top player, Kei is framed with a smile, together with other top players.

■be talked about 話題になる　■genuinely 副 心から　■no longer もはや〜でない
■longingly 副 憧れて　■from a distance 遠くから　■selfie 名 自撮り写真　■make public 公開する　■frame 動 (カメラなどの) フレームに収める

この2試合前のラオニッチ戦で勝利を納めたあとの記者会見では、「勝てない相手ももういないと思う」と日本語で発言し、話題になったことを記憶している人も多いだろう。

　それまではシャイで謙虚な男、というイメージだった錦織だが、全米オープンをきっかけに、自分の実力を信じ、それを臆せず表現するようになった。「自分は、憧れの眼ざしで一流プレーヤーを遠くから見る選手ではもうないのだ」、「エリート選手の仲間入りをしたんだ」と、心から思えるようになったのだ。

　その数カ月後に行われたATPワールド・ツアー・ファイナルで、トマーシュ・ベルディハ（チェコ）が出場選手全員と自撮りをしたときの写真が公開された。自信を持てるようになった心の内を表すかのように、錦織は写真の一番手前で、満面の笑顔を浮かべて写っている。そこにあるのは、かつてチャンに指摘された、アイドル選手のポスターを見上げる少年の姿ではない。トップ選手たちとともに自身もトップ選手の一員として、笑顔でフレームに収まっている錦織の姿だった。

Stay Focused

Chang says he had talked with Kei over the past couple of months about winning a Grand Slam, where it was going to be, how they could break through, and all these kinds of questions. Then it came down to each day and taking things little by little.

If you miss the tree for the forest, you will lose sight of where you are. Chang is worried that Kei gets absorbed in the whole and only focuses on that when he looks at it. Rather, he prefers to continue taking things step by step and match by match. The important thing is not what Grand Slam he is going to win. It would be better to think that he will acquire a Grand Slam title as part of a progression along a path.

Chang often says to Kei, "We're not done yet," or "Stay focused." These men try to focus on the present moment instead of worrying about the future. It seems that Kei also had this idea before he met Chang.

■couple of 2〜3の ■break through（難関などを）打ち破る ■come down to（結論などが）〜に至る ■lose sight of 〜を見失う ■get absorbed in 〜に没頭する ■rather 副それよりはむしろ ■along a path 進路に沿って ■instead of 〜の代わりに

気持ちを今に集中

　チャンは錦織と、「どうすればグランドスラムで優勝できるか」について数カ月間にわたって話し合ったことがあるという。どのグランドスラムで勝てるのか、どうすればブレークスルーできるのか。しかし結局のところ、物事は少しずつ、1日1日を過ごして達成していかなければいけない、という結論に至ったのだという。

　森を見て木を見ずにいたら、自分がどこにいるのかを見失ってしまう。チャンは、全体に目線をやることで、そこに気を取られすぎてしまうことを懸念しているのだという。それより、一歩一歩、ひとつの試合ごとに集中して取り組みたいのだ。どのグランドスラムで勝つかが重要なのではなく、ひとつひとつのポイントを積み重ねていった結果として、グランドスラムのタイトルを獲得できた、というのが、あるべきものの考え方だと思う、と話す。

　チャンは錦織によく、「まだ終わっていない」「今に集中しろ」という言葉をかける。これは、先がどうなるかを考えることより、とにかくこの一瞬に気持ちを集中させる、ということだ。これは、錦織自身もチャンと出会う以前から持っていた考え方のようだ。

Before Chang became his coach, Kei said in an interview in July 2013, "I'd like to enjoy this life, this moment." His career as a professional tennis player will probably last just 10 or 20 years at best. The heyday of his life as a player is limited. So, instead of looking ahead, he makes the effort for as long as he can, concentrates on now, and enjoys the moment.

[20] Positive Thinking

There is a distinctive feature about Kei's interview. That is, the words chosen and spoken by him are very positive. It seems he has a habit of looking at the bright side in any circumstances.

For example, in an interview after he lost to Cilic in the 2014 U.S. Open, Kei started off by saying, "These two weeks, I learnt a lot of positive things."

Also, in an interview during the ATP World Tour Finals of that year, when Kei lost to Djokovic, interesting remarks were exchanged:

■heyday 图全盛期 ■look ahead 先のことを考える ■distinctive 形特徴的な
■look at the bright side 物事の明るい面を見る ■start off by saying 開口一番〜と言う ■remark 图意見、コメント

チャンがコーチに就任する前の2013年7月、錦織はとあるインタビューに答え、「この人生、この瞬間を楽しもうと思う」と発言したことがあった。プロのテニス選手としての生活は、長く続いても、おそらくあと10年、20年。選手として活躍できる期間は限られている。だからその間、とにかく先のことを思い悩むことなどせずに、できるうちに思い切り努力し、今に集中し、今を楽しむというのだ。

物事をポジティブに受け止める

　錦織のインタビューを見ていると、特徴的なことがある。それは、選ぶ言葉、口にする言葉が、非常に前向きだということだ。どんな状況でも、ポジティブな面に目を向けるような癖がついているように思える。
　例えば、2014年の全米オープン決勝戦でチリッチに負けたあとの記者会見。錦織は開口一番、「この2週間、ポジティブなことをたくさん学んだ」と口にした。
　また、その年のATPワールド・ツアー・ファイナルで、準決勝ラウンドでジョコビッチに負けた後の記者会見では、とても興味深いやりとりがあった。

Q: You have made history for Asia so many times. We have very few Asian players on the Tour. You compete in the same sport with players from Western countries. You have differences with them, culture, language, food. Do you feel a little different to most of the players?

Nishikori: I don't know. It's tough to compare myself with other players. I don't know. For me it's easier to live in the U.S. and do a good practice. Traveling is not too tough, you know, for me. Yeah, I always enjoy this Tour. I can go to a different country every week. I was really enjoying this week, you know, in London. They have a good facility here. They bring whatever I want here. The restaurant is really great.

His mental toughness seems to be illustrated in his reply.

■make history 歴史的な偉業を成し遂げる ■tough 形 難しい ■facility 名 設備
■whatever 代 ～するものは何でも ■illustrate 動 ～を例示する ■reply 名 回答

記者:「これまであなたは、アジア（テニス）の歴史を何度も塗り替えてきました。このテニスツアーにアジア選手はほとんどおらず、あなたはたくさんの欧米人選手のなかで戦っています。文化、言葉、食事の面で、そうした選手たちといろいろと違うわけですが、自分はそうした選手たちと違うなとご自身で実感することはありますか?」

　錦織:「わかりません。他の選手と比べるのは難しいですから、よくわかりません。僕にとっては、アメリカの方が暮らしやすいし、練習もしやすい。ツアーで旅に出るのも、それほど大変じゃありません。僕はいつも、ツアーを楽しもうと思っています。今週は、ロンドンを思い切り満喫しました。設備もすばらしいし、必要なものは何でも持ってきてくれるし、レストランもすごくおいしいです。僕はいつも、その瞬間を楽しもうと思っているんです」

　錦織のメンタルの強さが、この受け答えに凝縮されているように思える。

There is no need to compare himself with other people. It does not matter if other players are Western or very tall. He just plays his tennis. Professional tennis players go around the world and have to endure hard lives. But he appreciates his given surroundings and just enjoys the moment in front of him. Since he left home at the age of 13, this mental toughness and flexibility have supported him while he stands alone on courts around the world with limited language abilities.

Kei's Goal

Kei's dream of "being the no. 1 in the world" came one step nearer to reality when he went to the U.S.A. at the age of 13. When he couldn't speak English just after he arrived in the U.S.A., and when Chang joined the team as a coach, he never hesitated to talk about his dream.

■not matter 大した問題ではない　■endure ～に耐え抜く　■surroundings 图環境
■come one step nearer 一歩近づく　■hesitate 動ためらう

他人と比べる必要はまったくない。自分以外の選手が、欧米の選手だろうが、身長が何センチメートルあろうが、関係ない。自分は自分のテニスをするだけだ。プロテニス選手は、世界中を転戦してまわり、非常にハードな生活を強いられる。しかし、与えられた環境に感謝し、目の前にある瞬間をただ楽しむ。こう思える錦織の強さと柔軟さが、わずか13歳で海をわたり、言葉も思うように通じないなか、たったひとりで世界中のコートに立ってきた錦織を支えてきたのだろう。

錦織の目指すところ

　子供のころ、「世界ナンバーワンになりたい」と思った錦織の夢は、13歳でアメリカにわたったときにひとつ現実に近づいた。渡米直後の英語を話せなかったころにも、そしてマイケル・チャンがコーチとしてついたときにも、「世界一になりたい」という自分の夢を語ることを臆さなかった。

Instead of setting the big goal of "being the world no. 1," he set more feasible goals like milestones showing the distance traveled in a marathon along the way to his final destination, and achieved them one by one. The first goal was to be a Top 100 player in the world rankings. The next goal was to surpass Shuzo Matsuoka's no. 46 ranking. He steadily met these targets, and Michael Chang's support enabled him to become a Top 10 player.

His goals for 2015 were to do well in the Grand Slams, maybe getting into the semifinals or a final, and to win a Masters (ATP World Masters 1000).

Japanese fans who saw Kei just one step short of victory in the 2014 U.S. Open want him to win a Grand Slam as soon as possible, and they believe he can do it. But Kei is more realistic. In light of his experience of reaching the final in a Grand Slam, he would have realized what it would be like to be a Grand Slam champion. You can savor the victory only after you play seven matches in a two-week tournament.

■feasible 形 実現可能な　■final destination 最終目標地点　■surpass 動 ～を上回る
■meet a target 目標を達成する　■one step short of ～の一歩手前　■in light of one's experience 経験を踏まえて　■savor 動 (経験などを) 味わう

錦織は、いきなり「世界ナンバーワンになる」という大きな目標だけを掲げるのではなく、マラソンの距離を示す標識のように、最終目標地点に向かう道のりのなかで、まずは自分が達成できそうなところから目標を定め、順にクリアしていった。プロになってから最初の目標は、まずは世界ランキングで100位以内に入ること。そして次は、松岡修造の46位を上回るということだった。これらを順調にクリアしていき、トップ10位に入ることも、マイケル・チャンのサポートにより叶えることができた。

　2015年の目標は、グランドスラムで準決勝か決勝に進むなどして、いい成績を残すこと。そしてマスターズ（ATPワールド・マスターズ1000）で優勝すること、とした。

　2014年の全米オープンで優勝を目前にした錦織の姿を見た日本のファンの心理としたら、今すぐにでもグランドスラムで優勝して欲しいと思っているだろうし、優勝できると思っているだろう。しかし錦織はやはり堅実だ。自分が実際にグランドスラムで決勝戦まで勝ち上がっていった経験から、グランドスラムで王者になるということがどういうことか、よりリアルに理解できたに違いない。2週間という長丁場になるトーナメントで、7試合も戦わなければその勝利は味わえないのだ。

In an interview with the foreign media in January 2015, Kei admitted that Japanese people may have higher expectations than in the previous year, but coolly remarked that he would need a couple more years to get more experience and get stronger both mentally and physically.

As for Grand Slams, he could not exceed his 2014 performance. In the Australian Open and the French Open, he did well but placed in the Top 8. He withdrew from Wimbledon due to injury. In the U.S. Open he was unfortunately eliminated in the first round. But in August he won his tenth victory on the ATP Tour, renewing his all-time winning streak as a Japanese.

Kei will surely attain his own dream that he has had since childhood and the long-cherished dream of the Japanese tennis circle of winning a Grand Slam in the next few years.

■as for 〜に関しては　■exceed 動 〜を上回る　■eliminate 動 〜を敗退させる
■all-time 形 史上最高の　■winning streak 連勝　■long-cherished 形 長年抱いてきた
■circle 名 [複合語で] …界

2015年1月の海外メディアとのインタビューで、錦織は日本での期待が去年よりも高まっているかもしれない、としながら、もっと経験を深めて、メンタル、フィジカル、あらゆる面でもっと強くならないと。それにはあと2、3年必要だろう、と冷静に分析した。

　2015年、グランドスラムに関しては、2014年の活躍を上回ることはできなかった。全豪オープンと全仏オープンでは健闘したもののベスト8。全英はケガのため途中棄権。全米オープンでは、残念ながら初戦敗退となった。しかし8月の時点でツアー通算10勝目をあげ、日本人史上最多記録を更新した。

　錦織はきっと、グランドスラムでの優勝という、自身の子供時代からの夢そして日本テニス界の長年の夢を、ここ数年のうちに達成することだろう。

Stimulating the Asian Tennis World

When Chang agreed to be Kei's coach, he had one thing in mind. As mentioned previously, there are only a few male Asian players who are successful in the tennis world. Chang thought that tennis in Asia would flourish more by turning Kei, a young, talented Asian player, into no. 1 in the world.

Among Asian female players, Li Na (China), who retired in 2014, has been the best. Her personal-best ranking is no. 2, the highest among all Asian-born male and female players. As for Grand Slams, she won the 2011 French Open and the 2014 Australian Open, which were also firsts for all Asian male and female players.

Now that Li has retired, no Asian players, male or female, are in the top rankings except Kei. This means that Kei is the best role model for Asian players who get training with the aim of playing around the world.

■stimulate 動 活気付ける ■flourish 動 繁盛する ■role model 他人の手本となる人物 ■with the aim of ~を目指して

アジアのテニス界振興のために

　マイケル・チャンが錦織のコーチを引き受けたとき、チャンには1つの思いがあった。前述した通り、テニス界で活躍しているアジア出身の男子選手は非常に少ない。しかし若くて才能に溢れたアジア人選手である錦織を世界ナンバーワンに育てることで、アジアでのテニスをもっと盛んにできるのではないかと考えたのだ。

　アジア出身の女子選手では、2014年に引退した李娜（リー・ナ）（中国）がこれまでで最強だろう。自己最高世界ランキングは2位で、アジア出身選手としては男女を通じて最高記録だ。また、グランドスラムでは2011年の全仏オープンと2014年の全豪オープンで優勝しており、こちらも、男女を通じて、アジア出身の選手で初めての快挙となった。

　李が引退した今、世界ランキング上位にいるアジア人選手は錦織をのぞき男女いずれにもいない。つまり、将来世界に羽ばたこうと夢見て練習に励むアジアの選手たちにとって、錦織が一番のロールモデルとなっているのだ。

Kei said that Li's retirement was a very sad thing because she had a tremendous impact on the Asian tennis circle. He said he was greatly encouraged to see that Li, an Asian player like him, fought worldwide and attained good results in Grand Slams. Kei said, "In the near future, I would like to be in her position. I hope I can give confidence to many Asian players."

This dream has come true in a sense—at least in Japan.

Matsuoka once explained the impact of Kei to the foreign media. According to Matsuoka, tennis has become more and more popular in Asia these past several years. When Matsuoka showed children a video recording of Kei when he was younger and trained at Matsuoka's camp, there was an immediate buzz. A top professional who plays around the world like Kei used to be in Japan, in the camp where they were now. Seeing the video, they realized that the goal of being a professional player doesn't have to be a dream. That dream might come true in their own life if they make the effort.

■impact 图影響　■come true 実現する　■at least 少なくとも　■buzz 图ざわめき

錦織は、李がアジアのテニス界に与えた影響は大きいため、彼女の引退は非常に悲しい、という。同じアジア人選手である李が、世界で戦い、グランドスラムで良い成績を残している姿を見て、とても勇気づけられたというのだ。「近いうちに、自分も彼女と同じ立場に立てればうれしい。アジア人選手がたくさん出てきて、僕が彼らに自信を与えることができたら」と、錦織は語った。

　この夢は、ある意味、すでにかなっていると言ってもいいだろう。少なくとも、日本国内においては。

　松岡修造が、海外メディアに錦織の影響を話したことがあった。松岡いわく、アジアでのテニス人気は、ここ数年でかなり向上している。松岡が指導する子供たちに、錦織が子供のころに松岡のキャンプでトレーニングしていたときの姿をおさめたビデオを見せたところ、明らかに子供たちがざわめき出したというのだ。錦織のような、世界を相手にトッププロとして活躍している選手が、かつてはこの日本で、自分たちと同じところにいたのだ。そんな姿を目の当たりにして、プロ選手になるのは決して夢ではないのだ、と子供たちは気づいたのだ。がんばれば、自分の人生でも現実になりえることなのかもしれない、と。

Alison Lee, ATP executive vice president in charge of ATP tournaments in Asia, says that the worldwide success of a great player like Kei is a good stimulus for Japanese and other Asian tennis players. He is not a player who is 2 meters in height; he gives other players hope that they might be able to do the same thing because Kei, whose build is similar to theirs, has gone this far.

Kei will continue to shape history in Japanese and Asian tennis circles and give us further hope.

■executive vice president 取締役副社長　■in charge of 〜の責任者である　■stimulus 図 刺激　■go this far これほどの成功を収める　■shape history 歴史を形作る

アジアで開催されるATPトーナメントの責任者であるATPエグゼクティブ・ヴァイス・プレジデントのアリソン・リーは、錦織のような選手が世界で活躍するのは、日本だけでなくアジア地域全体の選手にとっていい刺激になる、という。身長が2メートルもあるような選手ではない、体格が自分と似ている錦織があそこまでできるなら、自分にもできるかもしれない、という希望を与えているのだ。

　錦織は、これからも日本テニス界そしてアジア・テニス界にさらなる歴史を刻み、さらなる希望をもたらしていくだろう。

覚えておきたい英語表現

> There **used to** be times when he would throw in the towel. (p.144, 最終行)
> それまでは、ムリだと思うと諦めてしまうところがあったのだという。

【用語】 used to 動詞：（以前は）〜したものだ。

【解説】used to 動詞 は、昔はやっていたが、今はやっていないこと（過去の習慣）について述べたいときに役立つ表現です。上述の例文を見ると、以前はあきらめてしまうところがあったが、今は違うというニュアンスが含まれます。したがって、used to 動詞 が使われていたら、今はどうなのかについても意識するようにしましょう。

【例文】 He used to be waiting for the opponent's misplay. But now, he uses his forehand more. (p.148, 下から8行目)
これまでは、相手のミスをひたすら待ってしまうところがあった。しかし今はもっと自分のフォアハンドを使うようになった。

Kei used to look shy and humble. (p.152, 5行目)
それまではシャイで謙虚な男、というイメージだった。

> Two consecutive five-set matches **should** be proof that he has overcome his mental weakness. (p.146, 1行目)
> 2014年全米オープンで、2試合連続でフルセットを戦ったあの粘りは、まさにこうした精神面での弱さを克服できた証しといえるだろう。

【用語】 should：〜だろう、〜のはずだ、（〜すべきである）

【解説】shouldを見ると、「〜すべきである」といった義務の意味を思い浮かべ

がちですが、ここでのshouldは「〜のはずだ、〜だろう」といった可能性・推量の意味になります。私の周りのイギリス人と、仕事や難しいタスクなどについて会話していると、It should be fine.（大丈夫なはずだ）ということをよく彼らは口にします。

【例文】　It should be raining tomorrow morning.
　　　　　明日の朝は、雨が降っているだろう。

　　　　Q：How is your work?
　　　　　　仕事の調子はどう？
　　　　A：It is actually tough, but it should be fine.
　　　　　　実際けっこうきついけど、きっと大丈夫だ。

[参考資料]

英語媒体
Asahi Shimbun Globe
ATP world tour finals 公式HP
ATP World Tour.com
BNP Pariba 公式HP
Changing the Game（ニック・ボロテリー書籍）
CNN
ESPN
Guardian
IMG Academy 公式HP
Independent
Japan Times
NDTV Sports
New York Post
New York Times
Sky Sports
South China Morning Post
tennis.com
The National
Times
Tokyo Weekender
USA today
Vancouver Sun
ウィンブルドン公式HP
ゲイブ・ハラミロ公式ブログ
全米オープン公式HP

日本語媒体
http://tennis365.net
Tennis.jp
女性自身
東京スポーツ
錦織圭公式サイト記者会見記録
松岡修造公式HP
読売新聞
日本テニス事業協会機関紙JTIA News

English **C**onversational **A**bility **T**est
国際英語会話能力検定

● **E-CATとは…**
英語が話せるようになるためのテストです。インターネットベースで、30分であなたの発話力をチェックします。

www.ecatexam.com

● **iTEP®とは…**
世界各国の企業、政府機関、アメリカの大学300校以上が、英語能力判定テストとして採用。オンラインによる90分のテストで文法、リーディング、リスニング、ライティング、スピーキングの5技能をスコア化。iTEP®は、留学、就職、海外赴任などに必要な、世界に通用する英語力を総合的に評価する画期的なテストです。

www.itepexamjapan.com

[IBC対訳ライブラリー]
英語で読む錦織圭

2017年4月5日　第1刷発行

著　者　　松丸さとみ

訳　者　　バーナード・セリオ

発行者　　浦　晋亮

発行所　　IBCパブリッシング株式会社
　　　　　〒162-0804 東京都新宿区中里町29番3号 菱秀神楽坂ビル9F
　　　　　Tel. 03-3513-4511　Fax. 03-3513-4512
　　　　　www.ibcpub.co.jp

印刷所　　株式会社シナノパブリッシングプレス

© IBC Publishing, Inc. 2017

Printed in Japan

落丁本・乱丁本は、小社宛にお送りください。送料小社負担にてお取り替えいたします。
本書の無断複写（コピー）は著作権法上での例外を除き禁じられています。

ISBN978-4-7946-0470-5